MW00974124

Poke Bonnets and Denim Overalls

by

Peggy Howard Gwillim, M.D.

Bloomington, IN Milton Keynes, UK

authorHOUSE

AuthorHouse™
1663 Liberty Drive, Suite 200
Bloomington, IN 47403
www.authorhouse.com
Phone: 1-800-839-8640

AuthorHouse™ UK Ltd.
500 Avebury Boulevard
Central Milton Keynes, MK9 2BE
www.authorhouse.co.uk
Phone: 08001974150

First published by AuthorHouse 5/18/2006

ISBN: 1-4259-2921-4 (sc)

Library of Congress Control Number: 2006903102

Printed in the United States of America
Bloomington, Indiana

This book is printed on acid-free paper.

Table of Contents

It is the fault of men to let the things that have been

Go to waste, and in the unmeaning present,

Sink the past—Anonymous

Introduction

Recently I read, <u>Our Southern Highlands</u>, by Horace Kephart[1], which was first published in 1913, and last revised in 1922. Having been born and reared in southern Appalachia, I will admit that Mr. Kephart had us "pegged to a tee". There are only two criticisms I have of his very thorough work: (1) he erroneously concluded that none of us wanted to leave the mountains, even for economic gain, or a cleaner, easier way of life, and (2) he generalized about us as a people and failed to enable the reader to grasp the uniqueness of any individual. He does, however, credit isolation as the factor which enables each person to develop his or her personality to enhance survival of self and kin, and to learn to modify behavior to gain peer approval or to cope with adversity.

---

[1] Kephart, Horace, <u>Our Southern Highlands</u>, MacMillan Company 1913 and 1922, University of Tennessee Press, 1976 and 1984.

Since I was born in 1925 and left Appalachia in 1941, it would seem appropriate to present my observations in this time period which immediately follows that of Mr. Kephart, albeit in an area of the "Highlands" modified by the coal mining industry. The drama, The Kentucky Cycle, by Robert Schenkhan[2], published in 1993, which insulted every native born Appalachian during its brief tenure on stage, reportedly resulted from the author's weekend visit to this region and the reading of one book about this area written by Harry Caudill.[3]

It is hoped the material presented here will be more realistic than that of the aforementioned play. It is an attempt to show the people beneath the "poke bonnet" and "bibb overalls" which affected my life and moral values.

It should be added that Horace Kephart stressed the two greatest blessings Appalachia could receive would be good roads to get their crops and wares to market, and that those few natives who receive higher education should return to their homeland to teach. Neither he, nor any of us, realized how much World War II and the development of television would change this region forever. During World War II, ninety percent (90%) of those who could read and write left Appalachia permanently. Those who remained soon received TVA electricity and shortly thereafter a television aerial was installed atop the tar paper shack in which they lived. Now the tar paper shack has

---

[2] Schenkhan, Robert, The Kentucky Cycle, Penguin Books, 1993.
[3] Caudill, Harry, Night Comes to the Cumberland, Boston, Little,

been replaced by a mobile home with inside plumbing, and their songs, dress, and behavior now conform to their television menu. Even those who survive on welfare checks cannot be identified as different from a Georgia "red neck" nor a "Florida "cracker".

There is one other reason for my attempt to show Appalachia as it existed before World War II. I have many times harbored a guilty conscience for my failure to return to Appalachia to practice medicine, so this effort is a vicarious apology for my choice of an easier way of life. Actually, I vacillated for many years in my attitude toward Appalachia. When I first left this region, my diction and expressions, especially the word, "fixin'", subjected me to much ridicule from my new peers, and so anger for my upbringing appeared. Later, after I was socially and financially secure, I made several attempts to return to Appalachia to see if there were some contribution I could make to the region in which many of my relatives still resided. After one of these early returns I wrote the following poem:

> I weep for my egoless kin
> Reared like I, to feel no worth
> Teased and belittled in the outside world,
> No wonder you hide in the hills.

But by the time I had traversed the miles of rutted two lane roads to exit the mountains; memory of the return to my old school prompted the next attempt with poetry:

> I loathe the teacher who substitutes the twang
> of guitar and voice
> For readin', fact, and phonic
> Damn to her who says

"Live in your past of ballad and basket"
And creates another generation of no hope
A horde of wasted minds and unskilled hands
Doomed to hoe the hillside corn,
Never to dare an urban life,
Nor share the beauty of Bach or Van Gogh.
Shame on you teaching products of the mountain
scene
You exploited the nation's pity,
And took and took
to sit four years in a teacher college.
The maverick you have become
In your native creek and holler
Shows no pity for your peer's offspring.

The name of my home town and the names assigned to my relatives and acquaintances are fictitious. Since Fundamentalism is such an integral part of Appalachia, each chapter will receive a related title which would be sung in any Baptist church in this region, and each phrase will in some way be related to the topic.

Chapter I

Just As I Am

To get to my house take US 25 east to where the kudzu vine has taken over the mountain, turn left up a once paved state road and go until you've crossed over the Cumberland River and railroad track on the other side, then walk about a mile up the first hollow you see on the left and that's it. 'Course it was easier to go on the L&N train back then because you could relax on the green plush seats and watch families eat fried chicken and biscuits from a shoe box while the train chugged up the other side of the river from the road and passed by the Three Sisters which were cliffs that hung out over the track. Then five whistle stops later you'd be in my home town of Coalville.

Coalville isn't much to look at, especially after a spring flood. Most of the houses are four room squares painted white, yellow, or pale blue and they are stilted to the hillsides so the bottom land can be used for raising corn and a garden. The town itself is an "L" of three blocks to fit between two mountains and a creek, but if you get there before 10 a.m. there is something friendly about Coalville with smoke spiraling up from each chimney and a kerosene lamp glowing from each kitchen table. It's like every house is saying, "Come in and share our coffee, fried fat back, biscuits, and gravy." But maybe Coalville is nicer in early morning because the fog is still steaming up from the river and creek, and up at the head of the hollow the fog will have risen high enough that you can see the start of the narrow track that goes up to the mine, while the gaping mouth of the mine is still shrouded in white oblivion, and it's like that little track is a stairway to heaven, or at least, it seems to lead to a misty infinity of purity.

If you've got a little courage you can drive all the way to my house, providing the pot holes are not so full of water they drown you out, and if the 2x6"s on the trestle haven't fallen into the creek. You see, that was the railroad up to the mine at the head of the hollow and the woman who owns the mine and the road keeps saying the mine will burn itself out and she'll open it up again. She won't let the county floor the trestle to make a car bridge of it, and every time somebody nails down the two 2x6"s that you set your tires on to drive across, she has Mooneyed Martin, who works for her, come with a crowbar to loosen them. The half dozen families who have cars have gotten good at hitting those boards just right so it isn't often you see men with jacks and boards prying a wheel out of the crossties.

After you cross the trestle, that shack down by the creek belongs to Champy Joe. They call him Champy because he was quite a gambler in his younger days, and then when he got married he had so many children they said he was a champion at that too. You'll notice the house has no porch and some of the siding is missing. They're so low-down sorry they split it up for kindling. Each spring everybody expects the house to wash away in a flood anyway.

That next house with its yard full of cloths line from which so many sheets and every size of overall and dress flaps in the breeze is where the Keene's live. Mr. Keene is a holy-roller and Mrs. Keene dips snuff and when you meet them and all their twins she'll tell you all her ailments.

Up on the side of the mountain, where all the junk car parts are strewn, is where the Lilies live. They have lots of children too and their weather boarded house is so full of beds there is only room enough to walk sideways between them. The children don't have any closets or chests of drawers so the children who occupy each bed have their clothes hanging from nails at the head of the bed and each has a paper box under the bed to hold under clothes and items they want to save.

That lipid yellow house with the gladiolas in the yard belongs to the Leas. Their hog pen is next to our chicken yard but it doesn't matter as long as the breeze blows straight up the hollow, but when the wind changes I wish they'd go back to the mining camp where they once lived.

There's an empty house down the lane on the other side of the Leas. I'll be glad when it has rotted away because it has always been rented to the strangest people and some cruel sad events have occurred there. I'll tell you about it later.

I forgot to tell you about the most important landmark in the hollow--the spout. You were probably so intent on getting over the trestle you didn't notice the cast iron pipe coming from the bowels of the mountain. A two inch stream of the purest coldest water flows from it winter and summer, and that's where you learn about everything that happens in this hollow. Everybody knows when each family goes to get its water so if you want, for example, to find out from Mrs. Lea if her husband is scabbing this week you go with your buckets when you know she'll be at the spout.

Dad Beaver kind of ruined this flat area around the spout when he squatted here. He rigged up his goat cart and hauled that hump-back trailer about four miles and parked it here at the mouth of that worked out pony mine. You can tell the room he added to it was made from scrap lumber and discarded coca cola signs, but with the sixty-five degree draft that comes out of the mine, he has the most comfortable house in the summer of anybody in the hollow. It's unsightly but Dad Beaver lives alone and makes his living collecting scrap iron and lead to sell to Japan. Actually, he also does a favor to us all because he cleans up junk scattered along the river bank.

So come on in and sit under our big maple tree that my father transplanted here in 1920 on the day they started to build our house. You'll notice my mother's iris and the lilac bush are especially pretty this year, and that massive rambler rose bush covering the hill on the other side of the road she planted there to hide Mr. Lily's junk car parts from her view.

I expect you feel dwarfed by these mountains that seem to be as steep as the side of an Egyptian pyramid. One begins just beside the road and another behind you a scant two hundred yards away, but actually this is the wide part of the hollow.

Before you meet my neighbors and try to comprehend why they were so important to me you'll need to know something of my parents. My father is a direct descendent of the first settler in the county and he is the oldest of eleven children. My sister is quite interested in genealogy but probably has introduced more nobility into the family tree than it deserves, so I made up a story of my paternal family history which I think more nearly fits the family temperament: In 1790 when grandfather number four came through Cumberland Gap with two other families to claim land earned for Revolutionary War service, he must have begun to feel he had brought his pregnant wife and three children on a snipe hunt. Early one morning he sneaked away from their encampment at a salt lick, scaled the steep terrain and climbed the tallest tree to survey the countryside. Then after an hour of silent deliberation, when the camp was packed, he announced to all and his surprised wife, "We ain't goin' on with you'uns 'cause I done looked it all over and there ain't no plateau of grassy meadows like they said. There ain't nothin' but more of these steep tree-covered mountains and narrow valleys between. I reckon with winter comin' on, me and the young'uns better start fixin' fer it." So without further ado he directed the mule drawn wagon and his family upstream, chopping when necessary to widen the Indian path, and finally when he reached a point where the water was no longer tainted with the smell of sulfur, he decided this area was as good as any as long as he could find a site flat enough for a house and garden. He was basically a farmer and hunter and his skills as a craftsman were learned from the Cherokees. In fact, he credited their survival to mimicry of the Indians and always vowed the cave they settled in, and where his next child was born, was warmer in winter than the log house they later built and chinked. Truly, he soon began to feel he was lord of a kingdom once he had sired enough children to tend the land and he could become a sportsman hunter.

It must have been a hereditary trait that my grandfather never much liked responsibility. He would go off for months at a time to serve as cook for a surveying party from Virginia and came home mainly to see each new child and create a new pregnancy. My father managed the family and tended the farm from an early age.

Dad completed the eighth grade, which was all he could get in Appalachia, passed a state teaching exam, and saved most of his twenty dollars a month salary to go to college to learn how to teach. He never taught another day after he learned how, a fact which I began to comprehend after I was exposed to education courses in a teacher college.

When he returned from World War I he worked in a commissary at one of Henry Ford's mines, then he became a deputy sheriff before he began to dabble in politics while he worked for the state highway department. When I say dabbled in politics--Dad only tells what he wants you to know so I never knew what he did to earn citations from Roosevelt and a state governor. He never held an elected office, but around election time he was awfully busy and appeared very important. He let me cast my first vote when I was six years old, the only time I ever voted for Franklin Roosevelt, though Roosevelt was the family's god who ranked only slightly lower than the God at the Baptist Church.

Mother is a little more complicated. She is an import to the mountains from a lush farming section of the state. Her father was a crippled Methodist preacher but nevertheless was spry enough to fox hunt six days a week. Mother, the youngest and prettiest of eight children, went with an older sister, Atee, to the State Normal School and they both earned their way through school by sewing. Each summer a wealthy family from Racine, Wisconsin, would send them train fare to come to their home and do the sewing for the entire family. When they finished the teacher curriculum at the Normal School they both came to the mountains to teach. They had been here about three years and had heard about how handsome and what a good catch my father would be, so mother met his train when he returned from the war. When you get to know my mother you will soon realize her determination allowed my father little chance to escape.

Mother was a constant contradiction in that she must always decide if any deed was her Christian duty or what people would think if such and so were done or seen. The only taboo in her life which encompassed both motivations was sex. Sex was a sinful abashing act to which she submitted three times because my father loved children so much. I've always thought it was a pity she couldn't have ordered my two siblings and me from Sears Roebuck like she did her baby chicks.

The too often asked question, what will people think, and the redress that children were to be seen and not heard made such an indelible impression on me that I spent a quiet passive childhood and it was only with prodding in late adolescence that I gained enough courage to give an honest opinion to a peer rather than reply with what I thought the peer wanted to hear.

Mother had two pleasures in life. One was listening to Ma Perkins on our Atwater Kent radio and the other was getting dressed up in a long formal dress to participate in the ceremonies at the Eastern Star. The remainder of her life was consumed with frugality and doing her Christian duty. In fact, when the fetal me became a capitalized I, Mother's physical discomfort was transformed into the discomfort of "teaching me in the way I should go" so I would "not depart from it." So intent was she that we get an early religious education that I knew the story of Jonah and the whale long before I was introduced to Tom, Tom, the piper's son.

Actually, Mother was an enlightened woman for her era. I found a McCall magazine booklet on prenatal care hidden in an upstairs closet. And in that same closet of magazines she planned to read someday, I found another booklet on the feeding and rearing of children. My toilet training, table manners, nap hours, chore and play schedule were all contained within that booklet as rigidly programmed as if a computer had dropped out of the sky five decades prematurely.

But who of us is totally consistent, free of all phobias and neuroses, and unmarked by inadvertent influences of childhood? My Appalachian beginning may not have been idyllic but it provided me with motivation to achieve and the ability to laugh at my own foolishness.

That I should become an Obstetrician-Gynecologist at a time when a woman's prime function was to serve a husband and rear his children, or if she were undesirable, she might "make" a nurse or teacher, can only be explained by the events and influences of the people contained in this story.

Possibly a brief history of myself is in order. I finished high school at the age of fourteen, graduated from the state University at the age of seventeen, and spent a few months teaching health and physical education in a mining camp school. Then a most fortunate thing happened for my future, an aunt died after having her common bile duct severed during surgery. When the clan gathered for her funeral, her sister persuaded my parents to allow me to go with her to Detroit, Michigan, so I could make lots of money. I got a job in a pharmaceutical factory in their research laboratory, earned less money than my aunt who was inspecting screws, but the whole world opened for me. In less than a year of employment I entered a huge university in Cleveland, Ohio, where I obtained a master of nursing degree. Toward the end of that schooling I got the yen to go to medical school, and had been promised admission to that same school. However, that school changed deans in the interim and the new "boss" thought women shouldn't be doctors and steered me back into pharmacology. It was not wasted time because my horizon broadened, but it was not my primary interest. The following year I entered another medical school, had a part time job throughout my tenure in school, and only graduated eighth in my class. After a year of internship, I completed a residency in Obstetrics and Gynecology in a woman's hospital in Detroit, Michigan. Teaching, the private practice of Ob/Gyn, and my devoted husband occupied the remainder of my life until he died.

Chapter II

How Beautiful Heaven Must Be

If beauty is the negation of the pretty, then Coalville was beautiful. A sign posted on the highway declared it had a population of 901 and that figure hasn't changed even with the mass exodus during World War II. It is the flat land between Graveyard Hill and Happy Top and it contains two paved roads (one to link highway US 119 to the mining camps beyond Coalville and the other to avert muddy feet of the citizens en route to the post office.) There are five rutted lanes of about two blocks length which are bisected by the paved road and continue to one of the creeks, but it was the convergence of the creeks from the surrounding mountains which determined the limits and configuration of Coalville. As one looked down from Graveyard Hill it looked like a big tear drop and the joined Hooter and Happy Top-Tater Knob creeks ambled west for about a mile to enter the Cumberland River like it was a tear running down a wrinkled cheek.

In 1925, this incorporated town was the shopping center for six mining camps and it boasted of two groceries, two hardware stores, a bank which went bust in 1929, a shoe repair shop, two drug stores, two yard goods and ready-to-wear stores, an undertaker's parlor, a barber shop with the added bonus of a shoe shine boy, a doctor's office, post office, dry cleaner, and of equal importance, there was a widowed lady in a little shack on the Tater Knob creek bank who told fortunes. She used the pattern of coffee grounds settled in her always at hand cup to predict the appearance of a tall curly haired man who would come into the lives of all adolescent girls, and she only charged a can of pork-n-beans or a nickel cloth bag of Old North State tobacco with a packet of cigarette paper attached. Always she gave the assurance that life wouldn't always be as drab as that to which we were accustomed.

There were Baptist, Methodist, and Christian churches, and most times about three Holy-Roller churches. The number of the latter churches was dependent on the fervor of the snake handlers at any given time, because each epidemic of this demonstration of faith made the membership act like a hive of bees with two queens --they swarmed, and a new meeting place was designated for those who wanted no part of this risky rite.

Coalville got a movie theater in about 1932, but it didn't have a restaurant until 1935 when the county politicians introduced slot machines as a legal game. Yes, the restaurant sold coca colas and Nehi sodas, and the owner or his wife would make ham or cheese sandwiches but no hamburgers were served because they didn't have a grill. The primary enterprise of the restaurant was the row of slot machines along the counter. The coal miners loved those slot machines, especially on Saturday night. The few times I was allowed to stop at the restaurant for a Nehi cola after a basketball game I was always intrigued to see the miners convert script on future wages to coins for the machines (they received eighty cents for a dollar of script) and it was not unusual to see them lose fifty dollars during the length of time required to drink my soda.

The combined grade school/high school was a three story brick building on the hill beyond Grave Yard Hill and obviously was called School House Hill. It was about a half mile south of town and could only be reached by crossing a swinging bridge overlying the railroad tracks or following a wagon road across Grave Yard Hill and Simpson Holler before climbing a circuitous path up the near treeless knoll. The high school didn't have a football team until 1937 because there wasn't enough flat land for a playing field. When they finally developed a team they played alongside a creek in an area that had once been part of a mining camp about three miles away. The games weren't very well attended because no one really knew the game and it was a long walk to the field and very tiring to stand on the sideline to watch the game.

Coalville had a fire department for a few years until the building burned down. It served very little purpose because there were no telephones, so the quickest way to get the fire truck was to write a letter. Actually, the standard way to alert everybody to help with a fire was to fire a pistol six times, pause and then fire the seventh shell.

In 1935, one of our local politicians opened a Ford dealership and another tinkerer put in a filling station with a tank that required hand pumping the gas into the glass cylinder before emptying it into the car.

We didn't live in Coalville because there was only space enough for businesses, homes for the families of the business men, and the families of the three churches with paid preachers. The old maid school teachers had rooms or efficiency apartments on the walk up floor above the bank, and the school principal with his family lived in a flat over the post office. The unpaid Holy-Roller preachers lived up the "hollers" like the rest of us ordinary people.

Perhaps it is wise to digress at this point to describe the geography of the Kentucky mountains and just what a "holler" is. Instead of reviewing the uprising of Appalachia from the sea as is well depicted by Horace Kephart, I'll put it in the vernacular of a mountaineer. When the Creator made North Carolina he put too much baking powder in the cake he meant to bake, so that all the mountains there are round with a sunken-in middle at the top. When He built Kentucky He had the right amount of leavening in the mixture, but he erred by allowing a "cloud burst" to occur before all the dirt got settled. Consequently, the top of the mountains look like a razor back hog and the sides only swell with jutting rocks and cliffs with barely enough soil to enable the seeds of oak, beach, chestnut, maple, and some pine trees to take root. The hollows (always called "hollers" by the native born) were the less steep depressions near the bottom of the mountain sides and sometimes there would be enough flat land to create a fork in the mountain and the "hollers" would become the hilly tributaries of the fork.

The biggest advantage to living in a "holler" was space. In town, a family home had only enough room for a row of hollyhocks next to the house and a postage stamp of grass to reach the privet hedge next to the sidewalk, and in the back yard they could only have the out-house and a row of beans if there was to be any space remaining for the children to play marbles or spin tops.

Our place was up Hooter Fork. It got its name from the one black family that lived in a little blue house with an attached barn. Hooter earned a living by plowing gardens, and his wife, Aunt Sarry, did housework and home nursing for anyone who could pay fifty cents a day. Their son, Sharky, was the shoeshine boy at the barber shop. The people who lived in four room match boxes stilted to the side of the hill had a garden, and the pig they were currently fattening would be in a pen beneath the house. In addition, about three-fourths of the families had a milk cow which would graze on the hillside and along the road. My family was considered affluent because we had a two story house and five acres of land with garden and chicken lot.

The unique feature of Hooter Holler was the single railroad track which coursed up the flattest land straight up to the mountain which joined the ones on either side. The wagon road ran along side the track for about a quarter mile, crossed the track and followed the base of the mountain on the left for another quarter mile where it was necessary to ford the creek to get back alongside the railroad track beyond a trestle. About a half mile later there wasn't enough space by the track for a road, so one had to again cross the creek and continue on its left side to the end of the holler. After the mine burned out and the track was sold to the Japanese before World War II, everyone began to use the railroad bed as a road and the citizenry even put two sets of 2'x6' boards across the trestle aligned for the width of car wheels, so it could be traveled across. The lady who owned the mine and mountain objected to this arrangement even though she had bought a car and learned to drive it somewhat. She would have a sign at the beginning of the road which said, Posted Keep Out. Invariably the sign was used for target practice and finally kindling. It required a little finesse to stay on the boards to traverse the trestle, but there were still so few cars that if a car got off the boards, the young male population always obliged the driver with help to get the car over the trestle.

One could hardly think of beauty when considering the problems of sanitation in this heavily populated region. If the businesses had plumbing, frequent overflow of the septic tanks made the town malodorous. In the mile long Hooter Holler there were at least fifty houses with an average of six family members. All the houses up the assorted hollers which were adjacent to the creek built their out-houses at the creek's edge so that beneath the two holer there was running water. There were enough flash floods so that most of the time the waste was washed away, but during the dog days of August when we had no rain, the creek bed would advertise whether each family used corn cobs or Sears Roebuck catalogues for toilet paper.

I couldn't admit to any beauty in this utilitarian society until I was en route home on an L & N train at the Christmas vacation after my first term at the state university. Today it requires less than three hours to drive that distance, but in 1941, it was an arduous trek to get home. To go by Greyhound bus would have cost less and wouldn't have taken any longer, but to walk three miles from the highway in high heel shoes and carry a suitcase with chemistry and physics books inside made this undesirable. Besides, I'd only been on a train once before and had enjoyed it, and to have the added bonus of only a mile and a half walk on arrival made the additional three dollars fare worth while. I really splurged that evening while I waited for the train and bought a twenty five cent paperback book which turned out to be the first dirty book I'd ever read - The Postman Always Rings Twice.

Our country had only been at war two weeks but already the train depot was bedlam. I'd left my relative's home early because I had already washed their supper dishes and didn't want to risk their seven year old hellion tearing a hole in my silk stockings. In 1941, we felt we must dress up to ride a train. There was nowhere to sit in the white waiting room, but there were lots of things to see from my vantage point by the gate from which I would exit. Lots of men in uniform roamed around, and some were sound asleep on those hard benches, while a few couples were so entwined in farewell caresses one would think the male in uniform was en route straight to Germany to finalize the European war. Finally the public address system mumbled my train's departure and it was ever so good to settle on a green plush seat facing forward. The young couple who snagged the backward part of the seat promptly turned it forward and were so snuggled together someone else could have used the other half of the seat. The car was so crowded there were men perched on suitcases in the aisle so that the cross-eyed vendor who sold candy, chewing gum, sandwiches, and razor blades had trouble traversing it. The middle aged lady sitting next to me hid behind a book as soon as she sat down, and the crying babies were far enough removed they could be ignored. Knowing the ride from Lexington to Corbin, where I'd change trains, was five hours, I, too, settled into my paper back and soon began to blush. But after the two principle characters had gotten in and out of bed twice already, the third time was like pie in the face too many times, so my attention was diverted to the darkness outside the window and the sparse flickers of light in the occasional houses we passed. There were still three hours remaining in this leg of my journey when my feet became tight inside my pumps with three inch heels and I hated wearing my brown felt hat with a narrow brim and veil which hung down over my eyes. Oh how good it would be to have on my usual saddle oxfords and take off that hat and uncomfortable girdle so I could put my head back against the green plush seat and sleep. But, no, I must conform and pretend to be a lady instead of a teenager from Coalville, Appalachia.

While the train stopped to throw off and acquire mail plus passengers at every cluster of habitation we encountered I drifted into consideration of a problem which needed to be presented to my parents during this Christmas vacation. My transfer to the University of Kentucky from a small Methodist college in Appalachia, where I'd spent the preceding year, occurred because a relative, a bookkeeper for a nearby mine, had asked my father if I could live with his wife and children in their home in Lexington to be company for his wife and help her with the house and care of the three children in exchange for room and board. He said he refused to have his children go to school in the mountains and he wanted all of them to be exposed to the advantages of the city instead of the pettiness of a mining camp. The only thing I would not be allowed was to bring any boys to the house. My father only earned one hundred fifty dollars a month, and while we raised all our food, there were always taxes, electricity, and the tithe to the Baptist Church to pay, and I'd already used up all the money I'd gotten from selling my cow. To ask for a scholarship, even if a possibility, was like asking for welfare. Since I was still too young to be part-time employed in a restaurant or store, this seemed like a real gift from heaven to be able to live with the Smiths.

On the Saturday in September before I was to enroll in the University of Kentucky he picked me up in a spotless little Plymouth coupe and I kissed my parents good-bye. The eight hour drive was a nightmare for me. Mr. Smith smoked cigars continuously and talked constantly of only three topics: how mean coal miners are, how stupid mountaineers are, and how crooked all the county politicians were. Once we arrived at his Lexington home he became a different man. Miners and the mountains no longer existed and he became the all loving husband and father.

Sophie Smith proved to be the most blah, energy deficient woman on earth. When Mr. Smith was away she stayed in a long fluffy robe most of the day and rarely went out of the house. She always got up in the morning to bathe and dress the oldest child to go to school while I cooked oatmeal, eggs, and biscuits and tried to keep the two younger children from making a mess of breakfast. Most of the time she would keep the little ones entertained while I did the dishes and made the beds before I got on a city bus to go to school. All day at school was my routine even though I only carried twenty hours with three lab classes, so there was lots of time to go to the library or gym. I played on the girls' field hockey and basketball teams and my physical education class was fencing, so I had a good time for an hour or two every afternoon before it was time to face the home I despised. It was necessary to grocery shop, cook dinner and wash dishes before I could go to my room to study. Then all hell broke loose - all three children insisted this was their play time in my room. I'd scuffle with them for about an hour while Sophie sat in the living room and listened to the radio. She not only never spanked them, she only talked to them in playful terms. When I'd ask them to leave my room the real combat would begin. Janie would hide under my bed while Dev would open a book and make pencil marks all over the page. While I tried to entice the pencil away from Dev, Dennis, the seven year old, would enclose himself in the closet. Several weeks of experimentation were required before I learned to retrieve Janie from under the bed and hold her under my arm while yanking Dennis from the closet by his hair, and then use my free hand to twist Dev's arm to enable me to dump them in the hallway. Quickly I'd slam the door and sit against it until they got bored and went to bed. Most of my studying that term was done on the floor with my back against the door, but there was no desk and chair anyway so it didn't matter.

An event had occurred on Pearl Harbor Day which probably altered my relationship with the Smiths. A senior Ag student whom I occasionally chatted with in the library asked me to go with him to get a sandwich and then to a movie. It was an enjoyable afternoon but when we left the theater I told him I'd get the bus on the corner and thanked him for the treat. He insisted on riding the bus with me and accompanying me into the house.

Before my date could be introduced to the Smiths we learned about Pearl Harbor. It was a surprise to find Mr. Jones still at home late on that Sunday, but while the radio continued to report variations on a theme of the epic bombing, he talked about all the changes which we would face because of this international crisis. My date declared he must forego his last term of college to join the military promptly but Mr. Smith thought otherwise and stated bluntly that we should use the uneducated boys for canon fodder. The two Smith boys were already at war jumping from behind one chair to the next while shooting at us with their toy rifles. Janie climbed into my lap and struggled to get my glasses while Mr. Smith talked on and Sophie sat passively like a china doll. Finally, Mr. Smith announced he needed a snack before he started back to the mountains so he got all of them out of the room. My date moved a little closer to me and reached for my hand. I looked at the large mirror above the fireplace and saw the three children hanging over the banister in the front hall and Mr. Smith snarled into the mirror from the kitchen. I called this to the attention of my date and suggested he should leave. He got a little kiss outside the front door and a promise to meet him at the library the next day. Mr. Smith gave a grunted response to the half baked apology I rendered before going to my room to sit against the door and cry. My friend left word for me at the library the next day that he'd joined the air force.

Nothing was mentioned of this episode when Mr. Smith returned the following weekend, though I made it a point to be occupied elsewhere most of that time. It was during the following week that Sophie awakened me in the middle of the night because she was in severe pain and was vomiting. They didn't have a telephone so it was necessary to awaken the next door neighbor to call a doctor. She had eaten heartily of pork chops and gravy at supper that night so it was no surprise when the doctor announced she had a gall bladder attack. He could only give her a shot and pills for pain and advise her about foods to avoid because she refused to do anything until her husband came back the next weekend. The only way she could reach him now would be by telegram. For the remainder of the week my focus was to nurse her and tend to the house and children and only be at school when there were classes to attend. On Friday she assured me she was fine and since her husband should arrive before midnight there was no reason to delay my trip home for Christmas.

Maybe I dozed off for awhile for I became aware of a stir in the train with a continuous stream of children going to the water fountain and adults standing in line to go to the john. A glance at my $2.98 Ingham wrist watch from Sears Roebuck told me it was almost midnight and we'd soon be in Corbin where I'd have to wait another four and a half hours for the train which would take me home.

The few people who got off the train with me were soon gone and it was easy to envy the telegraph operator, ticket agent, and even the janitor because they were busy in those wee hours of the night while I just sat. There proved to be a clean segment on the roller towel in the ladies room so I could dry my face after splashing cold water on it, and the food counter in the white waiting room had ten cent hamburgers and nickel cokes, but that cut very little time off the long wait. There were few people to watch from that hard two board bench and after hiding my paperback in my suitcase so my mother wouldn't see it, I retrieved my chemistry book and was absorbed for about two hours. Oddly enough I loved organic chemistry and had already read way beyond the assigned chapter. It was all so logical and orderly and my aspiration was to change my major from Home Economics to a field major in science. Home Economics teachers made more money than science teachers because of the funding from the Smith Hughes Act, but it seemed it would be far more satisfying to teach some branch of science than to give classes in cooking and sewing. If my plea to change my residence at school proved to be easier than I feared, maybe I'd ask my mother if I could change my major. Finally my eyes wouldn't focus any longer and my feet didn't want to be walked on. By this time each minute had six hundred seconds in it and each departing train which was announced was a disappointment. When at last we few were allowed to board our train for the last leg of my trip, the seats were of woven reed, and instead of heat vents along each side of the car, there was a small square coal stove in the center and two seats on either side of it were absent. It was cold in that car so those of us who arrived early hovered close to the stove. The whole train consisted of a coal burning engine, coal and water storage car, mail car and three cars for passengers. Soon a young girl with an upswept hair-do sat down beside me and settled her crying six month old infant over her shoulder while she retrieved a bottle of water from a diaper bag. She recognized me about the same time I realized she had attended my high school. Her hair-do told me she was a Holy-Roller and that explained why I didn't know her well. For a time we talked of what each had done in the last year and a half and came up with names of students each thought the other would know. I even held the baby's bottle while she changed his diaper and she shared her shoe box of fried chicken with me after she got the baby to sleep.

This leg of my journey was to be only four and a half hours and the mere fact that the train was in motion invigorated my spirit. The train stopped for several minutes at Barbourville and several students I had known at Union College the year before stood by the stove and told me what a good basketball team they had this year. E.Stanley Jones, the nationally known pacifist, had been back to the college again and now all the football and basketball players were pre-ministerial students and wouldn't have to go into the army. By the time they left for seats and a snooze we had reached The Seven Sisters and this meant I was almost home. There was now enough daylight that the steep eroded mountain could be seen on the train's right and the white shroud covering the Cumberland River on the left. The conductor made frequent trips through the car to announce the numerous stops we made and when we finally reached Cold Iron the mountain at the head of Hooter Holler came into view so I was virtually home. When we slowed for Coalville my suit case was already in hand ready for exit. Nothing has ever been as warm and friendly as the swirling smoke from the chimneys of all the houses which appeared in my home town. The rail mail sorter who had once taught school in Coalville caught up with me and carried my suitcase over to town. So many changes had occurred in the less than four months of my absence, I couldn't help mention how quiet and prosperous everything looked.

My father and sister were away from home at work and my brother had already joined the army the year before, but my mother was at home to give me a big hug. After consuming some left-over biscuits and jelly and a glass of milk I went out to the outhouse and looked thoroughly at the holler. The sun had now risen over the mountain and burned off the fog. Still coal smoke spiraled from every house, and as I returned to the house, everyone who walked along the road stopped to speak and say how glad they were I'd gotten home for Christmas.

It was Sunday night before my parents discussed the problem of my living with the Smiths. It turned out to be no problem at all. My sister wanted to go to a business college in Lexington and if we could pay for an apartment and eat on forty dollars a month we could try it. At that moment we had the best parents on earth. Some day I'd make enough money to have water put into our house and then central heating so we wouldn't have to scorch on one side and freeze on the other while we stood before the coal grate, but aside from these two inconveniences this was the most beautiful place in the world. Heaven would have to really be lined with street of gold to be better than this.

Chapter III

When Doubts Arise

Coal was king in 1925 when I made my entrance into the rugged terrain of Appalachia. Each day, except Sunday, a coal train chugged up the hollow in front of our house to bring the empty gondolas to the mine at the head of the hollow and return with loaded cars of coal. The engineer always wore blue and white stripped coveralls and cap and a red bandana around his neck, and never seemed to tire of waving to children at each house he passed. Before I started to school in 1931, that era was gone, and by this time unemployed miners squatted on their heels around the "spout" while they spat and whittled and cursed the coal operators, Herbert Hoover, and the adverse weather.

My father was a deputy sheriff, but the stories of my toddling around the house with his pistol protruding from my diaper are not vivid in my memory. I do, however, recall sitting on a high stool with the bank teller while mother did her shopping. Suddenly in 1929, my $23 savings and in-town baby sitter were gone leaving that window barred brick building as forlorn as the empty dry goods store, hardware, and drug store that had once elated shoppers from six mining camps and our incorporated town of 1100 souls.

We were the only members of the Baptist church who had a bathroom,so every year when a furloughed missionary came to boost the collection for the Lottie Moon Fund, and each summer when the seminary in Louisville sent Vacation Bible School teachers, they lived with us while they lured us barefoot, unwashed, heathen children away from the mountains and river. What those "do-good" women didn't know until they were ensconced into our guest room was that we children carried the hot water from the reservoir on the Home Comfort kitchen coal stove to fill their bath tub, and hand pumped water from the well on the porch to flush their john. Water was not connected to the bathroom fixtures and kitchen sink because the pipes might freeze, and indeed they would have because I damn near froze each long bleak winter in that big unheated house.

My universe, before starting school at age six, consisted of a mother, father, older brother and sister, and Atee. Atee was Mother's older sister school teacher who lived with us until she married Dad's old widowed cousin. Even after she married she still came to our house every Thursday to mend our clothes and tell us how to manage our lives.

My geographic terrain was limited to a feather bed upstairs, a high chair in the kitchen, a maple tree in the front yard, the grassless perimeter of a rental house in the three acre garden, and a Sunday School room at the Baptist church.

The high chair was my throne for at least two hours each morning where invariably I was reminded to think of the starving children of China and clean my plate while I watched my siblings whimper and quarrel through preparations for school before they underwent Mother's inspection and kiss as they left each morning. Promptly on their departure, Mother would place a pencil, paper, and a card of letters and numbers before me to copy with my right hand while she washed dishes, swept the kitchen and started cooking soup beans. She was so intent on this project I soon began to feel she was resigned to my being a squinty-eyed girl, but she surely would change the curse of my left handedness.

It was a crisp day in March when I was five years old that my world fell apart. A family with a boy my age had recently moved into the garden rental house. Each morning after an hour of writing practice, the stubborn snaps of my coveralls were fastened and I was sent out to play with the new boy, Lloyd.(Blue coveralls with a snapped rear flap were standard play attire for both pre-school sexes at that time.) He shared my lack of inventiveness to create fun from the materials at hand since we were not allowed to throw rocks, wade in the creek, make mud pies, climb trees, nor wander off to the mountain. We hopped around for awhile to get warm and talked of what to do. Hopscotch was out because Lloyd thought it was a sissy game. Then a big gust of wind blew the nearby outhouse door shut. Without further comment Lloyd grabbed the projecting wooden latch of the door, bent his knees and rode the door opened and closed with each billow. Each time I tried to tell him our mothers wouldn't approve he would only grin and ask if I wanted a turn.

For several minutes I walked around with my eyes on the ground, unable to decide what to do and where to go. Then I spotted a group of small holes about the size of BB's in the clay soil behind the outhouse. These must be doodlebug holes I thought and squatted over them for closer observation. I wondered if it was true these bugs could be called out of their holes or if that saying was just another grown-up spoof like snipe hunting. I'd try it and began to call, "Doodlebug, Doodlebug, come out of your hole. Your house is on fire and your children'll burn up." My eyes stayed glued to the holes but nothing happened. I repeated the call louder and was so intent on those little holes I forgot about Lloyd swinging on the outhouse door. I added additional threats to these legendary creatures, "I'll fill your holes with water and you'll drown if you don't come out!" Then Lloyd squatted beside me and added his falsetto voice to my doodlebug calls.

Suddenly he ran away and there stood Mother with red face and pursed lips. She pulled my shoulder socket loose as she jerked me up and began to flail my bottom with her bare hand. She was breathing fast when she stopped and said, "You know better than to swing on the toilet door." When I insisted the culprit was Lloyd her voice became furious, "So I've lied then, have I?"

As soon as I'd said yes, I knew it was a stupid reply, for she said, "I'll teach you to accuse your own mother of lying", and she spanked me again with all her angry might.

With her first attack I'd been too startled to cry but now the sting on my buttocks and frustration made silent tears flow profusely. When she was spent and asked if I'd learned a lesson, it was no effort to say, yes.

With tears gushing from my squinty eyes I walked through a newly planted patch of peas, out the garden gate and down the railroad track toward town.   For a time I cried out loud but this failed to relieve the anger which roiled within me. The half dozen women stooped and holding the edges of their aprons of dandelions and poke greens which they were gathering from the sunny side of the mountain ignored me. I scooped up some gravel and threw each stone as hard as I could at each dandelion I passed and wished each flower I hit was the woman who called herself my mother.

Soon the realization that I had nowhere to go made me sit down beside the ditch. No one would want to take in an ugly five year old left handed girl just because she could tie her shoes and knew the multiplication tables through the fives. Then a new fear entered my thinking--God. "God sees all and knows all even when you don't say it aloud. He'll punish me for how I feel about Mother and to go to hell would be worse than living with Mother." But what if God is just another adult spoof like doodlebugs and snipes and Santa Claus?" The image of chained bodies writhing in the fiery furnace of an eternal hell soon made me decide the stakes were too high to question that tenet.

My attention was attracted to the edge of the ditch where a crawdad muddied the water as it backed into a hole and stared at me with its little cinder eyes. Skeeters flitted along the water's surface and intermittently would disappear when a tiny silver streaked minnow splashed by.

I was still contemplating God's cruelty in letting little creatures be swallowed up by bigger ones when Mz. Lily, from up on the hill, approached me carrying a biscuit with jelly spilling out. "It's way past noon and I figured you needed this biscuit more than Spot. Besides he got to lick the gravy skillet," she said, as she smiled and squeezed my shoulder.

"I'm much obliged, but I aint very hungry," I said and stood up to leave. The compassion in her eyes made me want to hug her little neatly aproned waist but all I did was look down to her size three tennis shoes which showed beneath her ankle length gingham dress.

"Why don't you take it anyway, 'cause you might get hungry while you build a little dam in the ditch to save those tadpoles that are sprouting legs." I took the biscuit and began to lick the apple jelly that spilled onto my fingers. She gave me a gentle knuckle to the head and added, "Reckon I better git on back to the house. But don't be too hard on your mammy. She jest can't stand to ever be wrong."

Mz. Lily rapidly climbed the hill, jumping from rock to rock to avoid the mud, while I gobbled down the biscuit and wondered how she knew so much about Mother.

By the time my father stopped his Ford to pick me up at five p.m. I had a foot high dam in the ditch to show him before I asked if he'd keep Mother from spanking me for having muddy shoes and a wet coverall sleeve. Then I told on Mother for whipping me for what Lloyd had done. His only reply as he hugged me was that I could go with him to hunt the cow that would soon be freshening and then mother wouldn't know how I'd gotten wet and muddy.

When we returned with the cow and had filled her stall with fodder my brother and sister were excitedly telling Mother about a school event. Dad turned on the Atwater Kent radio for the evening news, and I scooted to my room to master the snaps of my coveralls and wet shoe strings. By the time I climbed into the highchair and we were all around the kitchen table, I was clad in flannel pajamas and fuzzy house shoes and was only a breathing silent fixture in the room throughout the saying of the blessing and the slurped ingestion of soup beans, corn bread, onion, and milk.

I kissed each good night just as Dad settled into a rocker to read the county paper and Mother began to hover over my sister and brother's home work, while I ran to my feather bed to dream of a grown up life and independence.

One of the unappreciated advantages of a childhood of chores was the number of hours in which the physical self was occupied with the rote performance of daily duties but the thinking self was free to roam to the limit of one's flight of ideas. And since our small well-informed adult community was always beset with dire or feared to be fatal illnesses, it was natural that much think time was consumed in musing on these awesome acts of God.

An aura of infallibility with which we regarded the local medical doctor gave us a secure feeling, and if he failed it was attributed to the incomprehensible will of God. Yet there were several people in our hollow who either because of religious scruples or a basic distrust of anyone who had "truck with the outside world" would not avail themselves of diploma doctors and relied entirely on prayer, medicine show products, or passed down home remedies.

I was about seven years old when I became fascinated with something with which I had no acquaintance. It was my chore to clean my cow's stall every morning before going to school. And it was the habit of a young attractive wife of a coal miner to smile and talk a few minutes to me as she went to town to get her husband's lunch materials. Even in winter she seemed to perspire, and she had a startled look in her eyes, but the bulge in her neck had developed so gradually I thought it had always been there. I was leaning on a pitch fork to talk to her but she hurried by without even a glance at me. As I stared in amazement at her different behavior, I notice something with its legs tied to a ribbon around her neck. This was a school day so I couldn't wait for her return to look again at this strange appliance on her neck. I already knew there was no point in asking my mother or sister what it was, so after my evening chores were finished I sneaked up to where Mz. Lily was milking her cow to get the answer. I knew she always told me the truth.

According to Mz. Lily, it was a tree frog on the goiter of my friend and it had to stay there alive for six weeks for the goiter to be cured, but if it died, and it usually did, the goiter would kill her.

Each morning thereafter I was glued to the road waiting for my friend to pass and attempted to engage her in conversation or give her daisies or anything I could think of to enable me to get a closer look at the tree frog without letting her know I was staring at her. I wondered how it felt to wake up at night and feel that little frog jumping on your neck, and then I worried how she would feel if she woke up at night and found it stiff and dead, and to know that instant she was doomed. By the end of the first week I was so consumed with my friend's frog and her fate that I accidentally spilled the whole story at Sunday dinner. Yes, my parents knew all about it but it was such a stupid thing when people wouldn't go to a doctor, they didn't deserve to live. I asked if doctors always cured goiters, and my father cited, "there is never a never and never an always", to which mother added that most things were in God's hands anyway.

Henceforth I could not dally after cleaning the cow's stall and had to become dependent on the Lily family for my daily report on the status of the tree frog.

I still don't know if they tried to feed the frog during the three weeks it lived, but I do know that a hurried prayer meeting was called at the patient's house in an effort to soothe her panic. I had never seen a prayer meeting for the sick but I remembered hearing them one summer a couple of years before when a young woman who lived down toward town was having terrible pain from advanced syphilis. She screamed above the voices of the singers at the prayer meetings held for her until the doctor came and gave her a shot and then the ladies would leave for home.

The next day at school I met Little Eileen Lily at recess and she knew how to get up to Bootleg Hollow where my friend with the goiter lived and she wanted to see the prayer meeting too. We took a circuitous route across the edge of the mountain to get to a blackberry patch which was just outside the bedroom window of my friend's house. We squatted behind the briars to watch and listen to the six women in cane bottom chairs sitting around the bed. Most were singing a hymn but a few were praying out loud and would periodically jump up and yell and go through some gyrations before returning to a chair. My friend was pacing around the bed, pulling her hair or wringing her hands.

Little Eileen whispered to me as it was going on to watch a particular woman who was about to get the "Holy Ghost". I don't know how she knew but the "unknown tongue" she spoke while she was gyrating around the room was just so much gibberish to me. I saw my friend sit down on the lace medallion cover overlying the pink satin bedspread and as she folded her arms and looked up toward the ceiling with her wide startled eyes she called, "Lord, I'm in your hands now." Her mother-in-law came to her then with a pan of water, kissed her and suggested she rest while the perspiration was wiped from her face and her trembling hands were washed.

We stayed behind the blackberry bushes until all the women had left. I was still choked up and about to cry for my friend when Little Eileen said it was time to go. It was a quiet hike home and I knew there would be repercussions for my being late getting home from school, but I had so many things to think about I didn't even hear my scolding.

The prayer sessions continued three times a day with the faithful of their Holy-Roller church taking turns in participating, and after each session they would reassure the community she was getting better and would tell how many bites of food she had taken and how many minutes of sleep she had gotten.

Five days later when I was almost home from school I heard a car tearing down toward town with its horn blowing continuously.

I only got a glance at my friend's startled face gasping for breath in the back seat while her husband rubbed her wrists. By nightfall the family reported she was in the hospital and being treated for heart failure instead of the goiter. Later she was transferred to a medical center and twelve hours after surgery for the goiter, she died.

Of course, the doctors told the family they could have saved her if she had only come sooner, but my chore time was consumed with wonder. It was not until after I had finished medical school that I knew. I learned the haunting emptiness of a clinical mistake, a haunting that never goes away, that comes to plague when tiredness overtakes, and a haunting that comes in the midst of a triumphant hunch to add humility to one's congratulatory bows.

There were many other incidents of tragedy which occurred during my childhood in Appalachia which left me wondering about the rationale of the guiding hand of God, such as the annual epidemic of meningitis which occurred right after hog killing time. This was a foul smelling time of year because half our class wore small bags of asphidity around their necks to ward off meningitis.

I also had a fourteen year old classmate who couldn't swim, who jumped into the river on a dare from some of his friends and drowned. None of us liked him much because he was such a "show off", but his mother never got over his death. She had him exhumed three years later so she could see him again.

I had a cousin a little younger than I who always went along when her sisters and I went up into the mountain. In springtime she always dallied along because she liked the sour taste of "sheep-shear" (a small oxalis which grows around fallen trees). We all ate some of it, but that evening she got a stomach ache and vomited. The doctor who saw her thought she had been poisoned and gave her a big dose of calamel laxative. She died five days later from what I later decided was appendicitis, but the other thing I also couldn't understand was that her family buried the two dollars and change with her which they had given her to take her medicine, yet they were financially very hard up. I wished I had answers to some of these questions.

Chapter IV

He Walks With Me and He Talks With Me

Probably one's parents are the least known characters one meets in a lifetime, for the images they create when one is extremely young can only be modified slightly as one ages, and yet these two people are the most important factors which determine how one reacts to any given situation.

My father was a fourth generation descendant of the first settler in the county. Being the oldest of eleven children, my father had to accept a large responsibility in the family's affairs, and this alone should have made him a typical mountaineer. His speech was typical of all his crones except that I never heard him say "ain't", and while he never said "thank you", the phrase, "I'm much obliged to you" was frequently heard. The word "drekly" meant as soon as possible, and "fixin' was a substitute for preparation.

He became atypical after he had spent three years in the eighth grade and passed an examination to become a teacher. There were no high schools in the county at that time. While much of this part of his life is vague, I have the impression he taught school and saved his money to go to college. There is much ado made about his having a camel back trunk and riding horseback for twenty-five miles where he sold his horse and got enough money to go by train the remaining fifty or so miles to reach the college where he hoped to eventually study law.

I credit his mother's brothers with having influenced him to go to college because they were the most literate people in the county and several of them taught school. Probably it was only the era in which they were reared, but my paternal grandmother and four of her daughters could barely read and write.

In spite of my maternal grandfather having lived with us for a number of years, I didn't know him very well either. By all reports he had been an active fox hunter in his younger years, but to me, he was only an old man who chewed tobacco and spent most of his days in a cane bottomed chair propped against the porch wall, and his greatest concern was when it would next be time to eat.

My maternal grandmother knew how to sing "shaped notes", card linen, spin, weave, cook, and complain. During the eighteen years I knew her she enjoyed ill health and died at the age of eighty. By contrast, my paternal grandmother was an active, loving person who gave her all to her children and relatives until a stroke at the age of sixty relieved her of further obligations.

My paternal grandfather had inherited considerable land, could read and write, was well respected, and took politics seriously. Both sides of the family voted the straight Democratic ticket, which meant they were aligned with the south in the War Between the States. Even though he lived only a half mile away, I never really knew him. When our family visited him or when he stopped by our house, his conversation was always with my parents, so my knowledge of him was that he carelessly chewed tobacco, walked to town every day to whittle and tease with his contemporaries, unless he was miffed at someone or his candidates had lost an election. But after a few days at home he would return to town on the pretense of need to pick up the mail.

There are lots of gaps in my knowledge of my father's early life before he was married to mother. When I was about nine years old, a first cousin informed me Dad had been married before to a woman who lived in town and had a son about my age. She was a stupid woman and her son was just plain silly, and I accused my cousin of lying when she told me this. Unfortunately when I asked my Mother about it that evening she said it was true. Her excuse for the event was that he was very young and she wasn't a good wife so it didn't last long. It was then I learned he had acquired typhoid fever early in his marriage to her because she was too lazy to pump water from the well and he got the disease from drinking water she had brought from the creek. Apparently she didn't know how to take care of him so my grandfather practically moved in with them and saw to his needs during his prolonged recovery. His wife was so uncaring that she often stated to my grandfather that she wished Dad would die or get well instead of lingering on so long. The word divorce was never mentioned, but after Mother's recital of his illness I could understand why he didn't want to remain married to her, so my idol didn't develop feet of clay.

My parents never fussed but Dad was a bit of a tease. Many mornings during the summer when day light came so early, Mother would take time to play a few hymns on the old upright piano. When Dad came partially dressed downstairs, he would sing, "And every time I hear you play, I feel that I must dance."

I suppose by modern standards, my Father was a workaholic. In addition to a full time job, he always did a three acre garden, and always sang quietly while he worked, no matter how hot or distasteful the chore. Each morning of spring, summer and fall, after completing his morning chores, he would walk through the garden before dressing for work. Always, he sang in a low voice, "I walk through the garden alone, while the dew is still on the roses."

The Great Depression entered our lives in 1929, and it was then my father quit being a deputy sheriff working with the local revenue team, and became the boss of the state highway department. I didn't know why his change in jobs occurred until some years later when I ran across a transcript of a court hearing of two revenue officers and my father who were on trial for shooting a bootlegger. They were acquitted but the whole affair left a bad taste in my mouth for years and this knowledge left me perplexed. I did mention it to my sister some days later and she read the transcript too, but we both felt there was no one with whom we could discuss it, and so it was tucked away in the unused portion of my cerebrum.

As superintendent of the state highway department, my father did all the hiring and firing. Since unemployment was rampant at that time, there would be a line of men starting about four in the morning and by the time my father made his exit out our front door to start his morning chores, the line of men would be at least thirty people long. His first question to all of them was to ask who the man's father was and where did they live. But he talked to them while he milked the cow and fed the chickens. He would then return to the house to start breakfast for us all. Everybody worked six days at week at that time so it was only Sunday which varied and made the queue of men seeking employment endless. We soon learned the best way to avoid the continuous stream of people seeking work was to prepare a picnic lunch of fried chicken, potato salad, deviled eggs, and grape juice while we prepared breakfast, and by the time the chores were finished, it was time for Sunday School and church. We took the picnic lunch along to these obligations so that when church was over, we could set off in our car to spend the rest of the day surveying the roads, learning about the local flora and fauna from my father, and reading all the Burma Shave ads. The unpredictable aspect of each trip was a flat tire or sliding off a new road. All of us were required to pump up the tire or push the car back into the muddy rut of the road, but it created a change of pace and was exciting to me.

My father was a creature of habit so our lives were well regulated. When he arrived home at the same time every evening we knew exactly what he would do and what he expected each of us to do. We all ate supper together and then he would begin to read the newspaper while my sister and I helped Mother clear the table and do the dishes, while my brother brought in the kindling and coal and pumped a bucket of water. Each of us sat in the same chair every evening in a den where a coal grate was located so in the winter time Mother, my sister and I had red streaks on the front of our legs. When we were assembled it was time for the evening news on the Atwater Kent radio, then Amos and Andy, followed at Lum and Abner. At the end of this period of forty-five minutes, it was time for our home work and for Dad to peruse the newspaper more thoroughly. If one of my siblings needed help with a problem he would take care of it, and when we were finished with our school work he read to us for a half hour. I remember distinctly the first book was Huckleberry Finn and the second was Trail Of The Lonesome Pine by John Fox, Jr. Later he got into who-done-its, but we had gone through our collection of classics before we got to the low-brow stuff.

I was about nine years old when an unusual episode happened. Dad was at work, Mother was at a Missionary Society meeting, and my brother was playing with some friends in town. Suddenly Uncle Smokey, Dad's youngest brother, came staggering through the gate cursing with each breath. My sister and I were reading in the swing on the front porch and my sister greeted him warmly.

"I've come to get your daddy's gun. I aim to kill that SOB that says I'm a coward," Uncle Smokey raged as he started toward the door into the house.

Promptly my sister began to cry but I jumped out of the swing and stood in front of the door. "No, you can't," I said.

"Now little girl get out of the way so I can get the gun in his bedroom," he said.

"You'll have to fight me for it," I replied as I crossed my arms and broadened my stance.

By this time my sister was screaming and it was distracting, so he staggered toward her and told her he wouldn't hurt her. I could see he was moving his head toward me in front of the door. He made an attempt to push me aside, but I leaned into him and he was so unsteady on his feet he almost fell to the floor.

"If you'll go sit in the swing I'll get you some buttermilk to sober up on," I said. All the time my sister was screaming in a loud voice.

"I don't want to sober up. I want to kill that SOB in town," he said.

"Dad wouldn't want you to have his gun because you'd get killed or be sorry for the rest of your life if you killed him," I said.

"Guess I'll have to go on up the road to get a gun since you are being so hateful. You think your precious Daddy is the best man in the world, but I know things about him you don't want to hear. He's not as perfect as you all let on," he said.

I didn't answer and continued to stand in front of the door. Finally he turned and left so my sister and I ran into the house and locked the door. We both were shaking all over but only looked forward to our Mother's return from her meeting.

Mother was taken aback when we told her of the event. She relayed it all to Dad when he arrived. He gathered my sister and me into his arms and said we had done the right thing, but he was sorry we had experienced such a scare. I never asked him what Uncle Smokey was talking about when he said Dad wasn't perfect.

I thought Uncle Smokey was just jealous, and I didn't want to know anyway. Besides, Dad was the only one of six boys in his family who never drank, cursed, or smoked.

My sister and I shared an event with my father that we both remember as an epic occasion. It was during the governor's race and Happy Chandler, our candidate, was not expected to win. It apparently was my father's duty to deliver a Democratic vote for the entire county. The woman's vote that year was thought to be critical, and so he was told to take three women from our community to a campaign speech in Bardstown, which was a trip of about two hundred miles of mostly paved road. If we were to arrive there in time for the barbecue lunch and speech we had to leave home at 4:00 a.m. The reason my sister and I were selected to go was that we took up very little space in the car and we could help Dad with the ladies.

All was well as we sat off with one lady and my sister in the front seat with Dad, and I was wedged in the rear seat between the two fatter ones who were reeking of a very sweet perfume. We only had room for a few nibblings to consume time and hunger during the early hours. It required two hours to traverse the first fifty miles and my sister and I had led the ladies to behind the trees on the last big mountain to relieve their bladders. In another thirty miles or so we would be to a small city where there was a restaurant and flushing john. We stopped there and enjoyed cokes and a sandwich while Dad filled the car with gas.

The last of the mountains was in view and we were about a hundred miles away from our destination when a road sign signaled a detour. This was not an unexpected sight so we took it and continued as directed. Even Dad was perplexed when we happened onto another detour sign. Never before could I recall having been detoured off a detour, but so-be-it. Dad remarked that the road was getting worse all the time so hopefully we would soon be back on paved road. However, such was never to be. It got so bad and the miles so long that he would get out of the car to try to see what lay ahead. There was no turning back if we wanted to eventually reach Bardstown in time for the affair. Finally we were straddling a water stream, but in an effort to keep the car erect, it slid down one of the steep banks and broke the tie rod on the car.

We were so far out of civilization there were no people to help, so there was no alternative to walking. One of the fat ladies had on high heel shoes and so I became her crutch as we went uphill to look for any sign of life. It must have been at least five miles before we heard a cow moo, and so we went in that direction. Finally we saw a house and while we sat on rocks, we waited for Dad to find the inhabitants. Fortunately the housewife had come out of a tobacco patch to do some chores before the men came in for the day. He related our plight to her and asked her if he could pay her to fix us some food. She very kindly agreed and so the remainder of us advanced to a swing and cane bottom chairs on the porch. That was the best fried chicken, biscuits and gravy I ever ate.

While we ate we learned there was a wholesale truck which came by there every two weeks and it was due in that evening. Surely God was blessing us, for we were told the nearest road was ten miles away.

It was dusk when the truck arrived. Dad and the most important fat lady sat in the cab with the driver, so the driver's helper, two ladies, my sister and I sat among the bags of cow mash and rolls of tar paper in the covered truck bed. No, we couldn't sleep because of the rutted road, but we traversed the fifty miles back to a small city where a federal trial involving the recent coal mining warfare was taking place.

As fate would have it, the lady sitting in the cab with the driver and Dad was the wife of one of the coal operator's men who controlled their gun thugs who was on trial. She was sure he would see to our needs.

We climbed out of the truck in front of the fanciest hotel in that little city, and our fat lady asked the bell hop to find her husband for her. I washed the dirt and sleep out of my face and after the grownups had a cup of coffee, we got into the softest Oldsmobile I had ever been in. I slept the remainder of the way home and was able to do my morning chores before going to bed for the day. Happy Chandler won the election in spite of our not having heard his speech.

It was about two years later that his political cronies convinced Dad to run for county sheriff. The county was well known for its corruption, and the county court clerk had just been killed from a dynamite fuse set to go off when he started the car. Interestingly, the county always voted democratic in state and national elections, but for county affairs, it voted republican. In spite of this habit, Dad was expected to win because there were enough good people to elect him to clean up the county.

What he didn't expect was one of his closest friends who was a coal operator who would do him in. He literally had his henchmen to stuff a number of ballot boxes and thereby the county remained with the same crooked reputation.

It had been necessary for my father to resign his job on the highway to run for office, and in addition, he had used all of our savings to finance his run for office.

After the election, he went to see all his friends about a job, but none was to be had. In short order he decided he would have to farm to support us until a job was available. We already had a mule and turn blade plow, so in addition to our usual three acre vegetable garden, cows, chickens, and a couple of pigs, he cultivated a five acre hillside plot we owned and rented another hundred acres of prime land to raise more corn.

All five of us took part in this summer project and I can vividly remember lying on the living room floor to cool off and rest after lunch each day. We never went hungry but we didn't get fat either. The worst part of this belt tightening was finding enough money for the school work books required. We had to buy our own books in those days, but selling last years books for used one for the next year make it all come out even except for the extra workbooks.

I have no idea how much corn we sold, but I remember taking corn to the grist mill, and in exchange for a bag of corn, the miller would grind a bag free for us

This routine went on for four years before the coal operator who had stolen the election from Dad ran into him in the county seat shortly before Christmas. I'm sure Dad looked clean but seedy to the coal operator, and that must have prompted him to take Dad to a men's clothing store and buy him a new suit and tell him to come see him the next day about a job. The coal operator also sent a huge basket of turkey, fruit, nuts and candy to our home, and I cried because I didn't want to think of us as being poor. The remainder of the family didn't take that attitude so I couldn't refuse to take part in the eating of the alms.

Dad's job was night watchman at a mine until it was arranged for him to be employed by the state highway department. That remained his means of wage earning for the remainder of his working life. As he aged they even elevated him to appraiser and purchaser so he could work the hours he wanted.

Probably the most outstanding features of my father were that he was soft spoken, extremely kind, and had the patience of Job. He never complained even though he had been "gassed" in World War I and a respiratory infection each winter required him to make his concoction of bourbon, honey, and horehound candy to get him through the illness.

I can imagine how he must have felt when he and the whole family had traveled to Louisville to see me graduate from medical school. I learned on their arrival that he had all the symptoms of diabetes and that he had suffered from chest pain. The following morning before breakfast I took him to the laboratory where I worked and drew his blood for sugar. Sure enough it was markedly elevated. Before I graduated that night I had called a good Internist and arranged for his hospitalization the next day. My final argument to him was, "Dad, I know you still think of me as a little girl and that I can't know things like what's wrong with you, but I've gotten the best doctor I could find here, so after he checks you over in the hospital, if you don't need treatment he will discharge you."

His EKG showed he had already had an episode of a heart attack, but he recovered and lost some weight as he got his sugar under control. Even though he wasn't the perfectly managed diabetic he lived for twenty more years before a massive coronary thrombosis brought his life to an abrupt end.

While sitting in the front row pew at his funeral, I could only think, "Thank you, God, for allowing him to be my father."

Chapter V

Nearer My God to Thee

Coalville had thrived on being the shopping center for six nearby mines but in 1929, it became an array of empty stores and a boarded up bank. Only the post office, a drug store, three churches, an undertaker's parlor, an A&P, a barber shop with a one-armed barber, and a grist mill remained in operation.

Despite the overt signs of the Great Depression, nobody starved and there was a community comradery which has never recurred. Those of us who grew more vegetables than we could eat, can, or dehydrate, exchanged produce for labor or merely good will. Clothes were remodeled and recycled to younger family members or friends, but mostly we became the feed sack society. Sheets, pillow cases, slips, panties, and dish towels were all made from feed sacks, and if some Rit dye could be afforded, aprons, nightgowns and blouses could be made.

The churches, Homemakers Club, Missionary Society, the school basketball teams, Masons and Eastern Star thrived during this era as sources of diversion, and it was not unusual for a group to organize a community picnic where the adolescent girls could display their homemade black bloomers and middy blouses.

The mine at the head of the hollow had a methane gas explosion in 1928, so all the four-room cracker-box houses were abandoned along with the mine. But now that Henry Ford, US Steel, and Bethlehem steel were reducing their work forces because of the depression, families from mining camps began to move into our hollow into these sagging leaking structures which they would patch with Coca Cola and Nehi signs, cover the broken windows with cardboard, and split up the rotting porch for kindling. They could at least keep somewhat warm during our long bleak snowy winters and have enough space for a small garden and to keep a hog to kill for meat. Their families were so large they slept four to a bed and would not expect to have a "front room" with sofa and upholstered chairs from Sears Roebuck until the children were married and moved out.

It made no difference whether the family moved in from a truck, mule drawn wagon, or Dad Beaver's goat cart. If they had enough pride and initiative to repair and tar paper the roof, putty in windows, and build a new porch, they would be called upon and invited to the Baptist Church. However, if they just "made do", and didn't have enough "gumption" to even build a secure pen for the pig, they were assumed to be "Holy Rollers" and were left alone.

It was to this setting that Uncle Leslie appeared in town after a freight train passed through. Word to my family and grandparents had preceded his appearance because he had to stop off at the barber shop to get a shower, hair cut, shave, and shoe shine. What a dapper twenty year old he was when my sister and I ran to meet him coming up the hollow. Tall and slim with dancing blue eyes and a hat at a jaunty angle, he swept Karla and me up in his arms and swung us around until I was dizzy. Then he stooped to open his valise and withdrew two little straw Easter bonnets with a ribbon streaming down behind. After he placed them on our heads and arranged our hair just right, he said, "Now run and ask your Mother if I can have a glass of buttermilk before I go home to face the music."

Uncle Leslie had gulped down the milk and lit a cigarette before Mother said, "Tell us about college and what you're doing home in the middle of the spring semester?"

He gave a hearty laugh and tilted his chair back against the kitchen wall. "Dad was expecting a lot out of me when he bought me a truck full of clothes and put me on a train with enough money to last for a year of college. I really meant to enroll when I got on that train, but as soon as I began to see towns with street lights and all the homes with electricity, and knowing how hemmed in I've always felt here in the mountains, I started to wonder what it would be like to live in a city. I saw signs advertising picture shows and cars with rumble seats and some big ones driven by a chauffeur. Everyone looked so happy and proud. The Conductor didn't seem to notice I didn't get off the train where I was supposed to, so I didn't have to pay any more to go all the way to Cincinnati, but that was the last time I ever got anything for free." He stubbed out his cigarette, closed his eyes and sighed. "Maybe I'm looking for excuses, but I think I learned more than if I'd spent this year in college. For a little while I lived in a fine hotel and ate in fancy restaurants where the white coated waiters did everything but chew your food for you. I saw every movie in town and learned to dance, but let me tell you, it's when you start squiring girls that dress up every evening in pretty long gowns that your money really goes away." He lit another cigarette and continued, "I finally got a job loading barges on the river, but the company went bankrupt about a month later so I sold my trunk and enough clothes to get to Chicago where I'd heard the slaughter houses were still hiring men." We sat spellbound while he told of the skid row rooming houses where he lived, his assortment of jobs at the slaughter house, and of the immigrants with whom he worked. He told about getting a black chauffeur drunk so he could learn to drive a car, and told about the bread lines that extended for blocks, then about all the socialists speaking from soap boxes in the parks. Finally he even related an incident in which a fiftyish man jumped from a window and landed dead on the concrete beside him. It seemed his four month stay in that cold lake city was a trip to a foreign land without a happy ending.

I knew Uncle Leslie could never stay unhappy even though he had a quick temper and might throw a fist, so after warning Mother he might have to move in with us if Granddad threw him out, he walked out the gate and went whistling up the road like he owned the world.

It was the following morning when he came to get Karla, my sister, and me to take us up to his favorite lookout on a cliff above Graveyard Hill. He had shed his coat and tie but still wore a white shirt and his fancy panama hat. Always when he took us up the mountain he queried us about plants, trees, and the call of birds, but when we got to the cliff he sat down with his back against a scrubby tree and looked down at the coiling river and creek and the orderly patches of gardens alongside them.

Karla had found a little green snake and was teasing it with a stick while I leaned against Uncle Leslie whose arm was over my shoulder. After several minutes of quiet he told me he'd learned the hard way there was no place on earth prettier than this, but there ought to be more for a fellow to do here than work in a store or go into the mines and get killed. I dared to ask him if Granddad had whipped him for not going to college, and reminded him he could at least become a teacher if he got an education. After a chuckle he began to quote what I later learned was a Shakespearean sonnet, "When in disgrace with fortune and man's eye, I all alone beweep my outcast state—." Then he patted my head and said, "We'd best go back to the real world before the folks begin to worry."

For the next few weeks I only saw Uncle Leslie in town laughing with young men around the barber shop and occasionally under the trestle playing cards with a circle of men. It was well into summer when I saw a group of men kicking the tires of a shiny new car with a rumble seat. Uncle Leslie's grin as he stepped out of the gathering told me it was his car, and I glowed with pride when he opened the door for me to get in and bounce on the seat. After his younger sister, Flora, and Karla arrived he took us all for a ride and blew his horn and let us wave at everybody we passed. Chickens and mules were eager to get out of the way.

It was not until my family took a dried apple cake to my grandparent's house for its Sunday visit that I learned Uncle Leslie was in even more disgrace because he'd gone to work for the United Mine Workers and they had bought his car for him so he could be an organizer.

I heard Granddad exclaim that black gold warn't nothin' but the tool of the devil and warn't no reason to get it out of the ground as long as we had enough wood to burn. He sat in sullen silence chewing tobacco like a cow chewing its cud, then finally after he had spit tobacco juice over the porch banister he said, "Looks like Leslie ain't goin' to be no account. He spent all his college money and ended up a hobo, and now he's in with them flashy fellers that's come here to stir up trouble and get a bunch of people killed. Mark my word; they'll get more people killed than has been killed in the mines in the whole state since they opened the mines."

My father tried to be the peacemaker when he allowed Leslie would probably be a good organizer because he was respected and had a way with words. He also remembered how unsettled Uncle Leslie had been a few years ago when two of his friends got killed in a slate fall in the mines. Then there was another acquaintance of his who had a leg amputated on a track inside the mine, and even though he was only thirty-two years old, he couldn't work any more and had to go live at the county poor farm.

Grandma wiped the tears from her round wrinkled face and swept a white wisp of hair from her forehead before she said, "What will I tell my brother, Bentley? It looks like the money he makes from renting houses and selling burial insurance would be enough to keep his fancy wife in style so he wouldn't have to work for the coal operators and be the man to manage their gun thugs."

Again Dad was the peacemaker and promised to talk to my Great Uncle Bentley. He felt the mine conflict wouldn't be so great if the owners lived close by and knew how bad conditions were in the mines. Too many of the mine foremen wouldn't take time to have proper timbering done to prevent slate falls, and if the miners struck to improve mine safety instead of always asking for more money and bigger death benefits, the owners might be more sympathetic.

I knew to keep my mouth shut but I just had to ask why the government couldn't do something about conditions in the mines. Mother quickly went shush and threw up a hand to slap me, but Granddad and Dad began to laugh. Mother then asked what had happened to the senate investigator who had been here a few years ago.

Granddad chuckled again as he answered, "They rode him out of the county on a rail after he took up with a miner's wife. But the miner's wife took off while they wuz doin' this and ain't been seen since." They then began to talk about the crops so I went off to swing on a maple limb.

My father was a very punctual man. Even though he might stop at his cousin's drug store to politic or play a game of checkers, he always came home in time to help with the evening chores. Mother was inordinately quiet and tolerant during supper on a Monday night in mid September when Dad had not come home. We washed dishes, took the milk and butter back to the spring house (we rented space in an abandoned mine owned by a neighbor and this served as a spring house.), listened to Amos and Andy and Lum and Abner on the Atwater Kent radio, and still Dad had not arrived. Mother ironed while we did our home work and Mart and Karla had gone to bed without seeing Dad. Finally we heard slow footsteps on the porch and I heard the worried whistle he always used when he couldn't get the highway truck to crank up. A glance at Mother affirmed my fear that something awful had happened. His pale sweaty face and twitching muscles showed through his stubble as he went to kiss Mother and he sat down in an awkward manner with his left leg straight out. "Leslie got killed this evening," he said.

Mother could only utter ,"Hush!" before she began to cry, but as a six year old who has just learned her favorite uncle is dead, I could only shutter. Visions of Uncle Leslie floating up to heaven wearing his white shirt and jaunty panama hat and a big smile were interspersed with Sunday School pictures of tortured people writhing in the fiery furnace of hell while I watched Mother cry and Dad blow his nose. It was better to think he'd just gone back to college but would come back again changed as everything changes with time. It was just like a poke weed that dies in winter but comes back each spring changed into a thick green stalk with purple streaks and berries. No, God wouldn't take my Uncle Leslie away forever. Then I noticed a hole and blood stain on my father's left trouser leg. I poked my finger through and felt a bandage. I threw my arms around Dad's neck, kissed him, and began to sob. His arms were tight around me and I felt drops of wetness hit my neck, but he made no sound until I asked if he would be crippled now. How guilty I felt when I wanted to laugh after he told me he would get well.

We only heard a brief account of the evening events before he left to tell his parents. He and Uncle Leslie had been playing a checker game at the drug store with Cousin Doc and Cousin Bill, the owner of the store, looking on. Bill Bob, a greasy gun thug who now worked for the coal operators organization, but mostly hung around town drinking, playing poker, and cursing, entered the door and fired three shots into Uncle Leslie's back, and if Dad had not stood up when he saw the gun, the shot into the keys in Dad's left trouser pocket that ricocheted into his left thigh, would have gone through his heart. Cousin Doc jumped under the table and returned the fire but missed, and Bill Bob ran out the door and was seen outside running for the nearest mountain.

I had a hard time saying my prayer in bed that night after I thanked God for saving Dad. I went to sleep telling God I didn't blame Him for wanting Uncle Leslie up there with Him, so if He'd just let him stay jaunty and glad and strut around on those streets of gold, I'd go on pretending he'd just gone back to college.

On my way down stairs next morning the uncertainty of what to expect began to dawn. When I entered the kitchen it looked like preparation for a big church picnic was under way with platters of fried chicken, a lard bucket full of potato salad, tea cooling in a pitcher, Karla busy deviling eggs, and the aroma of a chocolate cake in the oven. No, we weren't bound for a picnic, the food was for Uncle Leslie's Wake. I also learned we'd been excused from school and Karla and I should take baths as soon as we finished breakfast, and should put on our pongee dresses and patent leather shoes just like we'd be going to church. When we were shiny clean and the ribs of our stockings straightened, we were ordered to sit in the porch swing and watch for Mr. Hartman's hearse.

It was about mid-morning when the long black vehicle with its black window shade pulled down slowly reached the trestle and stopped. Six young men who had been squatting on their heels by the spout came to the trestle to hold the 2x6's for the hearse to get across. It inched ever so slowly with its wheels on the 2x6's and even went slowly while it traversed the pot holes on the other side. The six men fell in behind the hearse and it was easy for them to retrieve a sack of "Old North State" tobacco and paper from a shirt pocket, light a cigarette, and smoke as they all ambled forward. As each house along the road was reached, its people dressed in their finest crepe, taffeta, gingham, or newest denim overalls joined the group, and each carried a container of food covered with a light bread wrapper, a jelly jar of hollyhocks or gladiolas, or a wreath of crepe paper roses. So many people had joined in that one mile trek in that narrow valley that I began to feel Mr. Hartman in the hearse was Moses leading the children of Israel through the parted Red Sea.

The sun did its best to belie the moroseness of the grown-ups as it appeared over the mountain at the head of the hollow and added a glitter to the dew wet pines and maples, but the adults continued to walk as if they never wanted to arrive. We children skipped, tagged and played hop-scotch, happy in a day away from the routine of school and anxious to sample the containers of such exciting aromas. The bonneted grandmothers with ankle length gingham dresses and buttoned high top shoes clicked their store bought teeth as they repeatedly exclaimed how awful for such a nice young man to be killed. The corseted matrons in taffeta or crepe gossiped between admonitions to their children to be careful with their clothes and the containers they carried. As more and more hands were dealt into the pot from each successive house we passed, and we saw the hearse stop to unload the coffin, anxiety and a sense of doom prevailed.

Despite our snail's pace we arrived just as the casket was opened in a dimly lit room with the shades drawn, the mirror turned to the wall, and only a 40 watt bulb dangled from the ceiling. Even the print of the Biblical Gleaners showed only its cardboard back so as not to reflect death. It all seemed to accent the deceit of the waxy rouged face and painted lips of the occupant of the satin lined casket. To see Mr. Hartman hold the arm of the old mother who fidgets with the seam of her tear soaked handkerchief as he ushers her to the side of her wasted son is worse than being chased by a giant from whom one can't get away. The smug expression on the face of the Undertaker seems to be saying, "Look what a good job I did", while I stand along side thinking, "Any resemblance in clothes, color, or character to the man I knew and loved is purely accidental." I left the room of death, placed the bucket of potato salad on the dining room table as if it were a sacrifice placed on the altar, and ran to the security of sunshine and the smell of grass.

I began to notice lots of adults who had escaped to a happier environment. Scattered all over that big green lawn were people shaking hands, groups laughing, exclaiming or confidentially gossiping. So in less time than it had taken us to inch along that one mile trek, the mass had been transformed from one of dejection to a comfortable prolonged picnic.

As soon as Grandma was put to bed and given a sedative, and my Father and Grandfather had gone off to the barn to check on the livestock, the Wake became a time for the older men to squat on their heels in a circle in the yard and leave a pile of whittled shavings to mark the center of their circle, while the broadcloth shirted fathers spat on whetstones and honed their pocket knives to sufficient sharpness to shave hair off their forearms, and for grannies to rock on the porch with smoke spiraling from their corn cob pipes, and to periodically voice, "What'd ye say", while they found words of wisdom to answer a question they had already heard. A Wake became a time to enjoy endless play interrupted only by an occasional wail from inside the house as new arrivals looked at the open casket. It was a time to flaunt superiority over the newly arrived fancy dressed cousins from the city and lure them into an abandoned mine to play hide and seek. A Wake became an occasion for people to consume enormous quantities of food and coffee, and for young men to go behind the outhouse and pass a bottle around, and for young women to go inside the outhouse to pass gas as if to accent the confidentiality of the gossip they passed on.

When the night time Wake is resumed following the obligation to evening chores, the children are sent off to giggle in beds shared with out-of-town members of the clan, while the women pleasantly chat, hug their arms, and drink coffee in the kitchen. The night time Wake is a time for men to pace in twos or threes along the shadows of the fence and stop to warm their gizzards from just a nip of the nectar of the Gods. Then in the pre-dawn hours they sit tailor fashion on the porch beneath the bare bulb and play gin rummy but do not bet as a concession to the dead. All the while millers are bumping into the light bulb and many fry themselves. The white ribbon and carnations attached to the front door have long been forgotten.

With the first light of dawn there is a universal yawn and stretch, and the echo of roosters announcing the day, and even the most bereaved come out to inhale the clear crisp air and see the rays of light peeping over the mountain top. They seem to gasp for the beauty of the morning before they return to the ugly within the house and the realization that one more day of this ritual is to be tolerated before they face the climax of it all. It will be a day just like the preceding one except for the slower pace of tiredness and increased quarrels of children who are just as strained as the adults and have had far too much togetherness with relatives whom they would otherwise ignore.

Unexpectedly, it was the second day of the Wake that became the day Uncle Richard, the youngest of the family, tried for the second time to identify himself as a man, or at least to numb his senses to the fear of it all, when he went behind the out house with the Esaus of the community to gurgle from the pocket flask passed around. After he was carried off to the hay loft to sleep it off so Grandma wouldn't know, the day proceeded in a familiar pattern.

The details of what had happened in the drug store after the shooting and the posse hunt for Bill Bob were now sufficiently embellished to consume much time at the Wake. I spliced together the assorted stories into a reel and added a bit of Tom Mix to the picture and this is the movie which remains fixed in my memory.

A solitary miner had just left the drug store after buying some Lydia E. Pinkham tonic for his wife when Bill Bob entered. He heard the shots and ran to the house of our constable, Hickory Leg, to tell him where the shooting was. By the time Hick had attached his leg and squeaked to the drug store it was filled with the curious who were exclaiming that Bill Bob was a half breed and you couldn't expect no better than that from him, especially since his mother had given him two first names. After Hick closed Uncle Leslie's eyes with pennies he stood around and spat while he watched the lead being removed from my father's thigh, and exclaimed how much he liked my uncle. He continued to talk to no one in particular as he added, "Fer's I know, Bill Bob ain't never done nothin' like this before, but I never did trust greasy fellers. I know he wuz flashin' a lot of money 'round town lately, but I never figured on nothin' like this." Then someone remembered seeing Judge Small go under the culvert with Bill Bob, and decided that must have been when he was paid to do the shooting.

The fervor of the on looking crowd was rising by the minute so when Hick declared there was no reason to deputize a posse until morning, the group insisted on starting the search as soon as they could get their rifles from home.

When my Father reached his parent's home that night, Grandma became rabidly angry and charged Uncle Richard to go kill Bill Bob and not come home until he had. Poor Uncle Richard, a skinny high school junior, my Grandmother's last menopausal fling, had never fired a gun in his life. Uncle Richard tried to insist the law would catch him and try him, but Grandma continued to rant and Dad tried to reason with her. When Granddad removed the double barreled shotgun from above the mantle and filled Uncle Richard's pockets with shells, Uncle Richard knew he had to go. Poor ungrown man, a loner who would rather read poetry than eat, a fellow who existed only to find beauty somewhere in his inconsistent world, and ignored the crude slanderous teasing of his classmates, but he straightened himself to his full five feet, three inches in height, heaved the gun over his shoulder, and marched off toward town.

Arriving at the drug store, he found Hick had already deputized a group of ten men and had appointed J.W. as leader. J.W. was a burley man with a ruddy face and was outlining their strategy as their family members watched them leave with more fire arms than were apparent at the battle of Bunker Hill. As they crossed the swinging bridge over the creek at the base of the mountain, their lanterns flashed like sparks from a campfire. Soon the lights became flickering fire flies as they fanned out among the trees as they scaled the steep terrain.

Uncle Richard hadn't said a word as he followed the lantern of JW, but as soon as his leather soled dress shoes began to slip on the mossy ground and fallen limbs, J.W. inquired why he had come with them. By the time they had attained the mountain top and stopped to rest, Richard had no doubt the entire group considered him a liability.

They fanned out again to traverse the ridge and look for footprints, but now their anger had been transformed into the banter of coon hunters. Uncle Richard could not find his way by moonlight and stayed discretely in the rear. Suddenly the silence was pierced with the call of a hoot owl, and they all knew this was the signal for them to assemble. Just below a jutting cliff where water trickled out was a fresh heel print. Their excitement grew as more and more prints were found along the forming stream. Cautiously they would intermittently stop to listen and then move stealthily forward a few more yards. This had gone on about an hour when a rustle was heard in the distance. Suddenly all guns were cocked and every man crouched in readiness to fire. Then out of the black they heard a thump and JW fired in the direction of the sound before he ran for tree cover. From behind them they promptly heard, "Hello there! What you fellers after?" They turned to see a moonshiner most of them knew.

The posse learned the moonshiner had seen someone pass a couple of hours earlier, but knowing nothing of the shooting, he had assumed it was a revenuer looking for his still, so he had climbed up along the stream to distract the possible revenuer.

The fervor for the chase was gone completely as soon as the bootlegger invited them to go help him "run off a batch of corn." They settled on large stones around the fire that leaped up around the large copper vat and watched the clear liquid drip slowly from the end of the coil into an earthen jar. The moonshiner returned from his hut with a gallon jug and handed it to JW. Before JW drank he mentioned he'd drink Richard's swig because he wasn't man enough to handle it. The rest of the group took up the banter so when the jug reached Uncle Richard he had to drink, even if killed him, and it almost did. Before dawn the posse had consumed two gallons of the white lightning and Uncle Richard was so drunk they had to carry him home.

The county sheriff sent out deputies with blood hounds the next day and they tracked Bill Bob to the county line. It was not until the following day he was captured and incarcerated in the adjacent county jail, and all agreed that was safer because my clan couldn't get to him there.

For the first time ever, I could have slept past the rooster's arousal on the third day of the Wake, but the two city cousins who shared my bed had hogged all the cover so I went to the kitchen to get warm. My parents were content to slurp their coffee in silence and offered no objection to my hovering behind the Home Comfort stove with my eyes on an opened book. While I pretended to read I thought about how much I wanted all the relatives to go away, and wished the neighbors would lose their sad faces when they patted my head. I wanted to ask what the funeral would be like but didn't dare. Instead, I conjured up an image of Uncle Leslie sitting up in his coffin with a big smile on his face, and waving good-bye as he began to climb up Jacob's ladder to heaven. No, I knew that wouldn't happen because there had been no miracles since John closed the New Testament with the book of Revelations. Somehow there were too many similarities between Jesus and Santa Claus, and I already knew Santa Claus didn't bring presents any more than Jesus responded to the want list I gave him every night in my prayers. As always happened when I wondered about the existence of God, the ingrained fear of the fiery furnace made me mutter an apology for my sin, and so I began to concentrate on my temporal needs like the growl in my stomach.

It was early afternoon before we again donned pongee dresses and patent leather shoes and returned to the Wake. Draped along the skimpy road shoulder above my grandparents house was the hearse with Mr. Hartman and more cars than I knew existed in the whole county. Mr. Hartman had saved a space for our car behind a big touring car just behind of the hearse, and from that car struggled a fat bald man who wore rose colored glasses. When he shook hands with my father tears escaped from beneath the big gold framed glasses and became part of the sweat that covered his round face. When I learned he was Great Uncle Bentley and the corseted perfumed queen who had alighted from the other side of the car was Great Aunt Isabella, I was amazed. She indeed looked regal in her satin dress and the circle of tail-biting animals around her neck. Even her small glasses on a gold chain attached to a glimmering pin on her dress added a note of opulence to her attire as they dangled over her abundant breasts. I was so lost in thought that we had reached the lawn before I became aware of the hundreds of people scattered on the grass and porch. They parted silently as we approached and it seemed we sat on the crest of a wave which was propelling us to the room where the open casket dominated.

It was a hot crowded room which reeked with the sickening sweetness of gladiolas and Great Aunt Isabella's perfume when Mr Hartman announced it was time for the family to take a last look at their loved one before he leaves his happy home. Loud sobs erupted as Uncle Leslie's ten siblings filed by. Granddad held Grandma to reach the casket and while she put her head inside the coffin to kiss him, I struggled with a tightness in my throat and turned to look behind the reversed picture of the Gleaners because the sounds filling the room were worse than I had ever heard. Soon Mr. Hartman called on a deacon to pray, a deacon I despised because his prayers were as long as a filibustering congressman determined to avert a vote on the nineteenth amendment. But on this day, his rambling served a purpose: it gave the family a chance to regain its composure and for Mr Hartman to get the procession organized in proper pecking order.

Ten elderly well dressed honorary pall bearers led the way and were followed by the real pall bearers, whose ties were alien to them, struggled with the coffin down the steps, across the bridge, up the hill, and into the hearse. Granddad and Grandma accompanied Great Uncle Bentley and Great Aunt Isabella in their big touring car, then our car was next, and on down the ages of the remaining siblings.

Except for the young men to hold the 2x6's on the trestle, while the slow moving caravan crossed over, the scene of the creeping cars was typical of rural America, and the only sign of animation was the shared communication of children fluttering dainty lawn handkerchiefs from the open windows.

When we arrived at the church, Mr. Hartman had cooled his sweat-drenched face and fastened the button behind his leather bow tie. He filed us and the flowers in perfect pecking order into the auditorium where the opened casket waited to hear its obituary and funeral. There were so many relatives the church was filled when only those through third cousins had been accommodated so the deacons had to learn how to open the sliding doors of Sunday School rooms at the rear of the church to make space for the friends to be seated.

Mrs. Hartman, the pianist, introduced the pitch of NEARER MY GOD TO THEE, but many times the words were replaced with sobs as the audience joined in. By the time the music score had been repeated for the third time and all the variations of ain't death awful, the minister had appeared from the security of his office, to stand rigidly stern and somber before the gathered mass. He didn't utter a sound until all was quiet and all the noses had been blown and handkerchiefs had been replaced in a hip pocket, and all mothers had picked up a funeral fan to blow away the hot flashes that he began with a reading from the book of John. The obituary came next and took as much time as the reading from the book of John, so I got bored after he called my name, and I created a nice reunion in heaven for Uncle Leslie.

Even this flight of ideas was arrested when the choir began to sing, Rock of Ages, but the family got one last big cry which didn't go away until old Mrs. Bonner's O-shaped mouth began singing The Lord's Prayer. Mrs. Bonner sang this at every church function of note so I didn't know if this was typical for a funeral, or just typical of Mrs. Bonner. I could not detect emotions of sorrow nor comfort from the sounds emitted from her O-shaped mouth in her mask-like face, and could only feel pain from the flat scratchy tones of her once soprano voice. By the time she had sat down and draped the sagging elephant skin of her arms over her crepe-covered foundation garment, I had decided her solo was really therapeutic, for now the clan looked emotionless and felt relieved that it, like the Wake, had been endured.

The minister arose again, took a deep breath and squared his shoulders to began, "We are here to beseech God, in his mercy, to find it in His heart to make a place by His side for our departed loved one, a loved one whose memory we will long cherish, and whose goodness we will long carry in our hearts. His beloved mother and father, brothers and sisters can live with the hope that he made his peace with God in the final moments of his life here on earth." I cringed as my thoughts flicked to create the two alternative scenes of the hereafter imprinted in the mind of every child of Fundamentalist parents long before he has even learned to eat with a fork.

The cousins around me had apparently tuned out the prophet of doom the same time I had for we began decorating funeral fans contained in the racks on the back of the pews. We printed alternative slogans for Mr. Hartman's "I aim to soothe in the hour of your bereavement." Then curiously, my attention was again directed to center stage and I heard the trembling voice of the minister say, "Oh, brother, you who have been so blessed with intelligence and you use it to sin; you who have been given friends and opportunity and you turn to drink. Oh, brother, don't sadden the hearts of your noble old mother. Don't let the circle of your fine upstanding family be broken in that home in the sky. Come to the Lord. He wants to save you."

This was the pitch which was already familiar to me from revival meetings, but I now felt incensed and angry when I sneaked a peep at Uncle Richard and saw his face hidden in a handkerchief and his shoulders shaking. I knew the preacher was aiming all his remarks directly to Uncle Richard. It just wasn't fair to proselyte when Uncle Richard was only there to honor his brother because protocol demanded it. In retrospect and with broader comprehension of evangelistic techniques of all Christian religions, neither is it fair for a man to be cured of appendicitis and won to God with the idea that it was the God- directed hands of the surgeon which worked the miracle of healing. The short of it all was that I seethed through the preacher's wind-down and the ritual of everybody filing by one more time to view the waxy remains of the deceased, and then the long slow labored trek up the eroded base of the mountain to a protruding clearing known as Graveyard Hill.

I couldn't watch the body of my endeared uncle being lowered into the ground. Instead, I looked farther up the mountain to the cliff where Uncle Leslie always went to commune with nature and do his thinking. If only he could be aware of his surroundings, he would be happy here.

Family members went to see my grandparents daily for about two weeks and always took something good to eat. They always helped with the evening chores and sat for awhile to pass the day. Always Grandma asked what they had heard of Bill Bob, and they assured her he was still in jail in the next county. It was a full year before he came to trial, and in the meantime the coal mining conflict had gotten more intense. Near the beginning a "scab" had been thrown in the creek and baptized in the name of the Father, Son, and John L. Lewis. Then there was a report of a group of "thugs" firing into a jitney full of union men and grazing the cheek of one of the men. Finally the governor of the state sent the National Guard into the county to referee the conflict and impregnate all the girls blossoming to maturity.

It was almost a year before the trial of Bill Bob occurred. School had not started so I could attend. Our court house was not the most elegant building in the county seat. They had all the windows open and had plenty of ceramic spittoons, but there was nothing to take away the body odor of the crowded onlookers.

It seemed the jury selection was based on how seedy and hard of hearing the assembled group appeared for them to be selected for jury duty. That took a day and a half before the first witness was called. For ten days I looked around the black wide brimmed hat of a cousin in front of me to see what was going on. Nothing made sense and nobody told the truth. Even Bill Bob said he wasn't even in town the evening Uncle Leslie was killed. And the money he was seen to be flourishing he said had come from Uncle Leslie in a poker game.

To this day I don't know who paid him to kill my uncle, nor how a sentence of five years in prison can atone for the life of one so dear to me, but the anger of my entire clan didn't enter into the minds of the twelve unschooled men of the jury.

There were some real marksmen in our clan and they had kept a record of when Bill Bob was to get out of prison. We all expected fireworks to occur at that time, but the form it would take was unknown to many of us.

Maybe there was some good in the inherited faith in the justness of the Supreme Being, the same faith which was brought through Cumberland Gap with our ancestors. As it happened, three months before Bill Bob was to be released, he was mutilated and killed during a homosexual assault by another prisoner.

I've also never known how the details of Bill Bob's life in prison in a far away city could filter back so completely to our isolated community when nothing of the outside world except the comings and goings of Franklin D. Roosevelt reached us. Yet this news reached our hollow and the mountains beyond like a raging fall forest fire. This is the climax I think of each time I hear, Nearer My God To Thee.

Chapter VI

Trust and Obey

Who is to say if the term I call justice is really just? And who is to say if what I call justice is unique to Appalachia, shared by urbania, or unique only to me? I am, however, sure that my slow deliberate musing through Plato's Republic after I moved to an urban life style has left me with no more concrete nor logical formulation of a course of action for attaining justice than that to which I was exposed in my Appalachian childhood. I have also come to realize that the acceptable course of the pursuit of justice in urban neo-America is far less expedient, far more costly, and sometimes less definitive than that to which I was accustomed.

It is safe to initiate a discourse on Appalachian justice with the idea that unquestionably God has the last word. I suspect the lead from many firearms has purposely erred to an extremity because of the belief that God will extract a surer retribution with far less fuss and bother than that required to aim a bullet toward extinction of one's adversary.

The idea that God also imbues all parents with divine wisdom and creates parental infallibility in child rearing is the second law of Appalachia. Beyond these two tenets I would be less adamant in insisting that the legal system derived from mother England was reserved for those situations in which one was still undecided as to the scale of value of the misdemeanor; whereas, a known misdeed worthy of human emotion demanded an independent course of action aimed at attaining an eye for the eye recently plucked.

In order to live in harmony with this rigid code of ethics, it became necessary to learn deceit. This seems incongruous with the professed forthrightness of a native-born Appalachian, but as will be seen in the chronology of events, deceit became the only means of withstanding the infallibility of parental authority. So profound was my awareness of need to pay homage to my parents that I suspect my first complete sentence in infancy was, "Honor thy father and thy mother so that thy days will be long upon this earth." New foods were gulped down because my mother knew I would like them, and even my toilet training was forced into awareness because mother knew I needed to go long before the sluggish signals from my autonomic nervous system told me.

At the age of five years, I learned that when Mother said, "So I've lied then, have I," I would get far less punishment to my back side if I answered in the negative, rather than the truth. Surely God had more interest in the fallen sparrows than in my honesty and the number of spankings I received.

Possibly it was my exposure to extra-familial affairs or maybe precocious rebellion which terminated my martyrdom and gave me the first sweet taste of just retaliation. My brother had given me a shiner after school the day his eighth grade teacher had asked three of us in the fifth grade to come before his class to perform feats of arithmetic, sentence parsing, and "Quiz Kid" type questions in history and geography to humiliate them. Naturally when my brother attacked I fought back despite my disadvantage in size and strength. Then Mother appeared on the scene and accused me of instigating the conflict. In a deadly calm, I remarked, "You wouldn't believe me if I said no and then you'd accuse me of saying you had lied. Since you'll whip me anyway, do it and then I want to talk to you because you can't listen now."

My brother ran while Mother's face reddened and her muscles tensed. As she began to strike, she screamed, "How dare you talk to your very own mother like that. Your mother who walked through the valley of the shadow of death to bring you into this world. After all the sacrifices I've made to bring you up right--the very idea!"

Still I stood soundless and as rigid as was possible against the posterior impacts. When she was satiated, I turned to face her and said, "You've always trapped me with your, so I've lied then have I. Since I can remember, you've made me lie in false confessions because you whip harder when I say you have lied. I love you because God says I must, but I want you to know that for over a year I've been marking off a calendar that goes until I'm eighteen, 'cause that's the day I'm leaving."

Her stunned silence denoted her comprehension, and as she tuned up to cry, she stated, "you don't mean it." That night she feigned a heart attack and I continued my deceitful martyred role in ministering to her, but thereafter, the phrase, "So I've lied then have I?" disappeared from our daily lives.

While the establishment of justice in our intra-family affairs was relatively simple, conclusions formed from the resolution of conflicts within the community appeared to be as devious as sex education. Throughout my life span in Appalachia, the court house was the vilest, worst smelling institution which could be imagined. Lawyers were considered liars and cheats and to even enter a court house required all the grit one could muster. It was made even worse when one considered the jury make-up of all trials, for there was no question they were the least educated, most slovenly, and most unreliable components of our citizenry.

An example of the conflict which occurred can be seen in Cousin Zack who had married into a family which had been involved in a feud for many years. As well as anyone could remember, the feud had arisen as a result of the court failing to award recompense for a cow they had sold, and the buyer swore the cow gave bloody milk. Consensus was that the buyer's size bespoke her total utilization of the milk, for the feed sack night gown she wore out on the porch each morning when she came out to empty her slop jar was composed of four feed sacks, each bearing the label, one hundred pounds net weight when packed.

Shortly after Cousin Zack got married, his father-in-law, the last male member of that clan, was ambushed. The culprit and his brother from the rival clan were kept in protective custody in the adjacent county jail to await trial. While there were no overt efforts to lynch or extract settlement ahead of the slow grinding process of adjudication, one sensed in our community a mass fervor of indignation and a thirst for justice which was not quelled by an early scheduling of the trial. It was as if the molten lava roiling beneath the surface of a volcano was already so liquid it could not separate its churning from the bubbles of its fury. This attitude continued through the migration of our community to fill every room for let and boarding house in the adjacent county seat while awaiting the selection of the jury and the trial. Neighbors and friends of the deceased sat beady-eyed and silent in the screenless court room while flies buzzed and flitted around the enamel spittoons during the days of jury selection. There was some voiced question of loyalty of the new bridegroom, Cousin Zack, because he would not accompany his bride to the court room. Instead, he loitered in restaurants, bars, and paced the sidewalk of the block around the courthouse. When court closed for the day, he would join her at the foot of the courthouse steps and they would go off to their boarding house for a quiet evening.

The morning the actual trial was to begin, the court house was so packed with on-lookers that people crowded through the doors and spilled out on the street. The two prisoners were handcuffed and were being escorted by three star badged officers carrying sawed off shotguns and wearing pistols. While the amassed crowd had given a wide berth to the advancing officers and prisoners, it was surprised to hear three pistol shots ring out and see the two prisoners wilt to the steps of the courthouse. There were at least a hundred people who should have seen who fired the shots, but no one did.

One prisoner died on the spot and rolled down the steps, but his brother was screaming and cursing from the steps where he fell. Later, an aunt who had a good position to see and hear everything going on told me how it ended. The mother of the boys climbed the steps in her ankle length gingham dress to where the wounded son lay. She sat down beside him and slapped his cheek as she said, "Now, Damn it, shut up and die like a man." He said nothing more and promptly died.

When our community returned home to continue its usual routine, it regarded Cousin Zack with such an aura of respect it was as if he had just returned from a holy war. I never heard anyone accuse him of doing the shootings, but it was not unusual to hear people say it must have been fifty yards, and it looked like someone was shooting black birds off a fence.

Cousin Zack took to his revered position with new-found sobriety and quiet voice, and was soon given the job of bookkeeper, cashier, and paymaster for a coal mining company. He kept this job for years but was fated to enjoy another moment of fame.

It had become standard practice for coal miners to strike when it was corn planting time and the opening day of bass season. It is not significant at this point to introduce the debate of justification for organized labor and its methods used in picketing. Suffice it to say that, despite the usual press depicted impression that the Appalachian acts in violence from his blind stupidity, it has always been my opinion that his violence resulted from the rage of frustration. He is smart enough to know that every time he enters that cold black cavern drifting for miles beneath the tree covered hills, that the creak of a supporting timber, the sharp snap of a slab of slate, or even the lightning flash of gas ignited from the carbide lamp on his cap that he may instantly reach eternity, or even worse, lie for days pinned beneath a slate fall gasping for the ever diminishing atoms of oxygen, daring not to fail to hope that the tons of debris will be removed or even a life-saving tube of air will reach him before he reaches eternity. With this awareness, is it any wonder that when the flat car bumps over the last seam in the mine track to return him to the light of the setting sun, he has an insatiable urge to feel, sense, laugh, and love, a yearn to live to the maximum of his limited capacity before the Big Ben alarm clock precedes the wail of the mine whistle to announce the hour of his return to another day of potential doom. His frustration is further multiplied by a respect for rank, but a disdain for, and envy of the product of rank. While he snarls at the drunken son of a coal operator who vulgarly displays the opulence of King Farouk, he is forthright in admitting he would do the same thing if he could. In fact, all too frequently he acts out a devil-may care pose in the process of feeding seventy-five dollars in nickels into a slot machine in a single evening "on the town".

The hazards, attitudes, and life style of miners were as well known to Cousin Zack and other salaried employee of the mines as they were to us all, but when men ban together for force, a new element is introduced. It becomes army against army, and plight of the individual is replaced by regard for the cause which will retain one's own snug familiar way of life.

When rumors spread that three trucks full of miners were being assembled just across the state line to attack with firearms, copper cables, and mine timbers, the salaried employees of the Scratch Ankle Coal Company knew it was time for defensive planning. Families of the salaried employee were sent out to all their friends and relatives to collect all available firearms. When anyone suggested a relic of World War I might be of no value because of "windage", the standard reply was always, "It don't make no difference. Cousin Zack will be using it and he can shoot anything."

After collecting a mass of guns, the wives of the salaried men projected their anxiety into the preparation of sandwiches, coffee, and desserts sufficient for a long siege. The Commissary door was locked and the salaried company men were collected in Cousin Zack's office in the rear of the Commissary, opposite the front door.

About mid-afternoon, the trucks full of picketers made their entry into the ghosted mining camp, and the only sign of life was an escaped child who was hastily yanked to security into a row house. The trucks were parked by a clump of trees near the Commissary and the tail gates were rapidly removed to discharge the noisy pickets rumbling anger and invectives on the tensed holler. Those men with firearms were dispersed to nearby cover of boulders or trees to provide protection for those with cable or timber who would charge the Commissary entrance. On signal, the roar from running feet and shouted determination marked the advance of the first wave of men to smash down the door and enter the commissary.

Cousin Zack stood calmly waiting with a rifle protruding through the pay window and a pistol on the counter by his left hand until the men broke through the splintered door and he began to fire. The startled few left standing made a hasty retreat to their companions hunched down under cover of their trucks and the trees. Then a committee advanced with a white handkerchief to remove the wounded and dead from the Commissary, and Cousin Zack replaced the first rifle and selected another for the next assault. This wave was larger than the first, and again Cousin Zack mowed them down as they entered the company store. He never took his eye off the entrance, and only spoke to his loaders to say, "Take this 'un, give me another." When the second siege was over and the white handkerchief was waved to precede the removal of their dead and wounded, Cousin Zack noticed that some of those who had returned to the cover of the trucks were slipping forward on either side and he yelled for pistols. He became the surgeon with a hand outstretched waiting for a hemostat even while the other hand was firing a pistol. Then it was over. Even before the white handkerchief was displayed for the third time, they all knew it was over. He stood with the pistols resting on the pay window ledge watching the removal of the slain and wounded. He broke his sobriety of many years with a request for a nip of moonshine which he instinctively knew would be in the hip pocket of each of his men. By the time the trucks of the bleeding defeated were loaded and retreated down the rutted road, Cousin Zack had drained a half pint bottle and was thirstily gulping from the second flask. He gave no order to be at ease or break camp, but when he was satiated with the clear colorless corn, he began to recite the one-hundredth psalm. His loyal assistants carried him to the company owned boarding house to sleep it off, while the grateful company owner and his friends began their celebration in the Boarding House kitchen.

Interestingly, while there was a thorough investigation of the years of conflict resulting from the unionization of the mines and millions of tax-payer dollars were spent with the court room trials which netted only hand slapping for a few of the less important participants, there was never one mention of Cousin Zack and the invasion of the Scratch Ankle Commissary.

When Cousin Zack's wife and only child met premature deaths from cancer, there were a few who rumbled that God was reaping retribution for the deeds of his past, but when it was learned that the cancers had a hereditary pattern, there were those who remarked that even without feuding , his wife's family was destined for extinction anyway.

With the knowledge of Cousin Zack's valor and the family's pride in his accomplishments, it would have been concluded that attainment of justice was a family responsibility, as was preservation of life and health. It could have been surmised that only misdeeds by unknown assailants would be left for final resolution by God, for honor demanded human effort to extract recompense for the offended member. To this day, I'm not sure this wasn't better than that which resulted from the horde of missionaries who perennially swarmed into Appalachia to reform its people into a tribe of helpless inadequates who stood hungry, cold, powerless, and uncomfortable until the government came with command and commodities, or the grim reaper interceded. I blame the Fundamentalism missionaries for the dissolution of the clan because it takes very few quivering voiced sermons about standing naked and alone before the All Mighty to make one crouch in fear and shame. One then becomes so fearful of the Holy x-ray eye or radar beam that penetrates one's very thoughts and that could potentially send him to the eternal fires that he becomes obsessed with individual initiative to preserve himself in the awesome hereafter and forget about his obligation to his kin.

By the time the missionary invasion showed its effect I was grown and working for the summer in a small hospital which was owned and operated by a coal mining company. I needed money to continue in medical school.

The serenity of a Sunday afternoon was disrupted by a loud commotion outside the hospital where I worked the night shift. At least a hundred people preceded the arrival of two bleeding shocked men on stretchers. I advanced to the hall where the stretchers were stopped and noted that the badge marked man had a blood stain in the pit of his stomach and three small black holes adjacent. The other man had only one penetrating hole in the left side of his chest and a whistle could be heard with each rapid breath.

The ever increasing crowd of on-lookers was eager to relate what had occurred, so I learned that the wife of Clem, the man with the chest wound, had called the company policeman, Zipp, because he was drunk and beating her up. When Zipp arrived at Clem's home in Chewing Gum Hollow, Clem grabbed a butcher knife to defend himself and Zipp tried to take it away from him without drawing his own gun. A number of the friends of Zipp had gathered at the house across the creek to watch the conflict. The combatants had wrestled from the kitchen to the porch before Clem suddenly freed himself and fired three shots from Zipp's pistol. Zipp doubled up and was holding a hand over his stinging abdomen but yelled out, "Kill him in the name of the law!" One shot rang out from the onlookers across the creek and Clem fell.

The loudly weeping wives of the victims could be heard in the distance before their self appointed ushers parted the mob in the single hall of the eighteen bed hospital to advance them to the sides of their wounded mates.

When this hubbub had started I wasn't even on duty and was clad only in a house coat. But those few of us charged with responsibility had decisions to make and procedures to be carried out, even if it is nothing more than throwing the spilled salt over the right shoulder.

By this time the surgeon had arrived and the superintendent of the mining camp had installed himself at the nurse's desk to get control of the milling crowd in the hall and control the telephone. The surgeon directed that Zipp be put on the operating table for immediate surgery and I had been sent to obtain the operating pack and supplies for the operation. I had deviated my route to pass by Clem and apply adhesive tape to his chest to stop the whistle in his breathing.

Suddenly someone grabbed the lapels of my housecoat and lifted my feet off the floor. "Now look, by God. We don't aim to stand around here and let him die. We want something done!" he shouted. I promised to tell the doctor promptly and he released me to return to the operating room.

When I reported to the doctor what had happened he became so upset he left the operating room to discuss the matter with the mine superintendent. Now the operating room contained Zipp, his wife, his mother, and the Baptist preacher. The scene which followed was one I had never seen before, and it despoiled my youthful aseptic rigidity as well as cast indelible shadows on the humaneness of the God of Fundamentalism. It was a scene which could never occur in the present day of complex rigidly regulated medical centers which have been so accused of the dehumanization of patient care, but as I attempt to objectively compare, I suspect the medical center atmosphere would have afforded Zipp his life, whereas we failed.

Zipp lay strapped on the operating table covered with cotton blankets except for the display of the three black dots and the dried blood on his abdomen. His wife wept loudly while Zipp clung to her hand and restlessly squirmed beneath the table straps. His mother stood nearby clutching her purse to her bosom. While tears rolled down her weathered face, she prayed softly, over and over, "God, please let him live. We need him so bad, especially now that they are going to have another baby."

The preacher laid his gray sweat stained felt hat atop my sterile instruments and advanced to the operating table after he commanded the withholding of the morphine so he could save Zipp's soul. Then putting his hairy hand on Zipp's cold wet shoulder, the preacher began, "Zipp, you're a might sick man and ye might be mortally wounded. They's a heap of things ye need to say so's they can get on with yer operation. Reckon they's enough witnesses here fer ye to say if you want your wife and younguns to have ever thing you left behind." Zipp nodded and answered yeah as he appeared to be drifting off to sleep. The preacher raised his voice another ten decibels and shouted as he shook Zipp's shoulder, "Zipp, do ye want'a name the baby your wife is carrying now?" Loud sobs were heard from the wife and the dozen relatives now standing in the operating room. Zipp shook his head and tightened the grasp on his wife's hand. "Now, Zipp, I know you've been a good man, but you ain't never been saved. Ye know that being a good man and a good father ain't going to get you into the kingdom of heaven, 'cause the Bible says unless you accept God as your personal savior and come to Him believin' His only begotten son, Jesus, died on the cross to save you from sin, and that it's easier for a camel to go through the eye of a needle than for a unsaved man to have eternal life."

Zipp continued to squirm on the operating table with his eyes closed and the preacher continued to yell at him, but it wasn't until Zipp nodded assent that the preacher shouted, Amen, and began to pray. He told God that Zipp wanted to be forgiven of all his sins and that he would forgive Clem for shooting him.

I slipped out of the room during the shouted marathon of prayer, frustrated by the realization that the fleeting time had already greatly lessened the probability of Zipp's recovery. I learned too that Clem had been taken to the county seat hospital where a doctor was waiting to operate on him. One member of Clem's family had been sent back to notify us that the family was coming back to get those of us working on Zipp as soon as Clem's operation was over.

Finally Zipp's operation got underway and we were so absorbed in hemostat, suture and retractor that we didn't realize the hoot owls had already quit hunting for the night. I quit counting lacerations in the intestine when it reached thirty-five, for I had never seen a patient to recover from more than that number.

When we moved Zipp to his bed, I was the only professional nurse left on duty, and I saw a group of four star badged males clad in overalls and lumber jacket squatting against the wall in the hall spitting tobacco juice to the opposite wall. These men I learned were sent from the next mining camp to protect me through the remainder of my solitary vigil of the night. Busy with the care of tubes and faithful to the recording of clinical observations, I bid good night to the departing remainder of the medical team, and ignored the escape of the lawmen to the hill behind the hospital where they would greet the day refreshed with a nip of the nectar of the gods.

The exhausted family of Zipp had been put to bed in the hospital and the hospital cook had just arrived to start coffee and breakfast when Zipp slipped quietly away from existence.

The legal tomes of Appalachia do not contain a case labeled, The state vs. Clem because Clem's family had come to Zipp's house even before the funeral and asked to be forgiven. Besides, Clem was paralyzed from his waist down but the United Mine Workers would pay for his rehabilitation.

A couple of weeks later I accompanied the mining camp doctor to Clem's house to change his dressing. On top of the family Bible on Clem's bedside stand was a 45 caliber pistol. I said, "Clem, I thought you had turned over a new leaf and would be a good man from now on."

"Well, I have," he said, "but a man would be a God damn fool to lay here and let someone shoot him down in cold blood."

In a society of clan against clan, or God against man, who was to compose the membership of the police system, and why was it not respected. One of the answers lay in the realization that the only ones who sought this job were those who were otherwise unemployable. There were a few exceptions to this rule, but when one considered the rewards for this office was a two dollar a day salary, the use of a set of pearl-handled pistols, and an unlimited supply of ammunition, it was no wonder that the office seekers were usually young bucks with pent up anger who used this job as a means of settling personal quarrels. His average time from swearing in to Wake was two weeks. On the first Saturday night, he settled the score with his enemies, and the second Saturday night, the clan of his enemies settled the score with him.

It was standard practice for our family to go to Sunday School early so we could learn who had gotten killed the night before. This practice came to a halt when some of our citizenry got together one day over a game of Rook and decided we needed a strong fearless, mature man to fill the office of city policeman. It should be someone who could be respected for his integrity and bravery without need for flashing a gun. Obviously, they had someone in mind when one of them remembered having heard Mrs. Oliver complaining about Oral having to be gone all week while he worked in the logging woods. They had only to ask old Judge Small to ask him to take the job and they would go along with the old crooked judge on this mission to express their support and gratitude.

When the delegation reached Oral Oliver, his massive frame so dwarfed Judge Small that Oral's smile did not return words to the judge's trembling adams apple, so a member of the delegation had to state their business. Oral sat in quiet deliberation for awhile before he turned to Judge Small and said, "Now, Judge, if I take this job I ain't standing for no one not getting a fair trial. And if I arrest someone with the evidence on him I don't aim to see him get acquitted just because you and his daddy is mixed up in some kind of deal." The judge squeaked out comprehension and approval while dropping his head from view of the wry knowing smiles of the delegation. Then Oral turned to the delegation and added, "And I'm telling all of you that if one of your younguns is caught tom-cattin' around and breaking the law, he's going to get treated just like everybody else. I jest ain't going to stand fer ye tryin' to beg me off."

Even in retrospect, it is impossible to depict specific episodes or comments which occurred after Oral Oliver pinned the city's badge on his shirt that created awareness that he was a giant of goodness. While his voice was gruff, his words were affectionate, and while his bulky size enabled him to crush effortlessly, his gentleness was in evidence as he nudged truants back to school, and his disdain for deceit showed in his sternness in dealing with petty thieves. There was one episode in which he arrested a hungry demented boy in order to provide a full meal for him while he was in jail. The characteristic which attracted most of us small children was his habit of standing outside a grocery with a foot propped against the step as we came from school and had stopped to look wishfully at the kites, tops, biff-bats, or balls in the window. After a cordial greeting he would ask each of us about school that day, and on some occasions he would award a penny to the child most successful in replying to his questions.

For months we were without stimulus for early arrival at Sunday School and the town became so quiet the newly opened theater began to show romance movies on Saturday night.

We even became a clean city because the arrested drunks were shackled together and made to sweep the streets and clean out the one storm sewer before they were released on Monday morning.

It was not until the day Oral failed to escape the line of fire that the delegation who had asked him to be the city policeman was struck with qualms of conscience. It was when they went to tell Mrs. Oliver about Oral's death that they remembered Oral was a professed atheist. They now felt guilty of having expedited his trip to the fiery furnace.

The preacher selected by the family to preach the funeral whined throughout the three day Wake, worrying about what he could say at the funeral. But of Appalachian funerals, to me, it was the least barbaric and kindest funeral I had attended.

On the day of the funeral a delegation of American Legionaries marched along wearing their blue over-seas caps, white leggings and gloves, and an honor guard from Fort Knox was in full dress uniform and carried rifles. The closed casket was draped with the American flag, so one could sit comfortably listening to the strains of funeral songs and visualize a warm smiling face above the massive frame of a man instead of a waxy face with eyes asleep and shrouded with the sobs of Nearer My God To Thee.

Reportedly, the widow Oliver had great difficulty in carrying out Oral's requests found on a yellowed page in his locked foot locker because her neighbors insisted he had written it when he was too young to know what he wanted, but when his buddy from the trenches of World War I arrived, he strengthened the resolve of the widow, save for the already requested preacher.

Possibly the preacher was subdued by the atypicality of it all since he made no effort to save souls during the sermon. Instead, he read a brief obituary, recited the third chapter of John, and followed with the briefest sermon he ever made. "Oral wuz a good man who served his country and fellow man in war and peace. If he had died in the war, we would have said he was taken into the bosom of Abraham 'cause he died to keep us free, and I reckon it's the same thing gittin' killed doin' his job. Besides don't none of us know what was really in his heart, and he was such a good man that I sorta think he loved the Lord whether he knowed it or not. Now, let us pray." When he had completed asking for God's comfort to the family left behind, the funeral march accompanied the exit from the church.

At the grave side, the army friend stepped forward and in a beautiful baritone voice demonstrating perfect control of diction and emotion as he stated, "In honor of my friend, I will now share a thought he gave to me long ago, a thought I promised to share with his friends gathered at his death." After a brief pause he recited, "The day, immeasurably long, sleeps over the broad hills and warm wide fields. To have lived through all the sunny hours, seems longevity enough. The solitary places do not seem quite lonely. At the gates of the forest, the surprised man of the world is forced to leave his city estimates of great and small, wise and foolish. The knapsack of custom falls off his back with the first step he makes into these precincts. Here is sanctity which shames our religions, and reality which discredits our heroes." Then putting the card at which he had barely glanced into his pocket, he added, "My friend lives in us all. His joy in the day was contagious, his exemplary valor was a model for which to strive, and his love for and his faith in the goodness in man humbles us all." He stepped back to salute the boxed coffin, a stance which he maintained through the drill and three shot volley of the honor guard.

There were interesting remarks overheard as we made our way down the nettled path from the cemetery on Tater Knob, but I continued to enjoy the remarks of Emerson heard from Oral's friend.

I never knew what punishment had been rendered for the man who shot Oral.

Chapter VII

This Is My Fathers World

Peg Leg, our constable, didn't have a degree in sociology, psychology, nor penology to serve as a foundation for his judgment. I'm also quite sure he didn't have a poll of public opinion to guide him in the most epic decision of his long political career. He did, however, have the advantage of several days of think time because the tempo of rumors spreading through the school and into the hollows was no less than that expected from the unprecedented arrival of a carnival in the dead of winter.

It was the dead of winter, that endless span of time after the Christmas sled runners have become bent, and the intrigue of steamy exhalations has long been replaced by pondering if one would ever be warm simultaneously front and back again. The raw bleak short days are overshadowed by the long depressing nights, and the memory of the smells of spring and Easter vacation are so remote as to be doubted they will ever occur again. But while it was the dead of winter, it wasn't a carnival which was being rumored. It was a snake handling.

As an adolescent sitting atop a rough hewn bench in the last row of an old store-front church watching this spectacle, it was as incomprehensible as voodoo and as pathetically funny as an old Buster Brown silent movie. My years of ruminating on these episodes have evolved some perspective, so that now the participants in this demonstration of faith are no longer animals who have just lost their prehensile tails in exchange for a limited vocabulary, but human beings limited by the inability to read and write, so there is nothing but faith in one's father to guide one's behavior and tenets.

One of the participants and probably the most typical of the Holy-Rollers was Slim Smith who was the umpteenth son of an old settler. Slim's father had eked out a living from 50 hillside acres of corn. The corn was quietly deployed into his vat camouflaged from view by a cliff overhanging a stream trickling circuitously down the mountain. Slim's father had been respected for his honesty and skill and trusted because he never worked his moonshine too fast. His many sons were an economic asset to him in tending the eroded corn patch, slopping the razorback hogs, and helping at the still when they were working a batch. The only schooling Slim got was when he wasn't needed at home.

Even though they lived in isolation, they enjoyed a steady stream of customers to their house, and on Saturday they all went to town to buy supplies, whittle and spit, and bring a few jars of moonshine from beneath the hay in their wagon to sell.

When Slim got big enough that his pappy "couldn't whoop him no more", he left home and got a job in a coal mine. He lived in the mining camp boarding house until he met a girl at the scrip counter one day and liked her looks. A few weeks later they got married. Even though her last name was Smith already, they assured everybody they weren't any closer kin than third cousins.

Slim became a conscientious husband and father after "The Lord took my first little girl with the Summer Flux to pay me back fer lustin' after the thangs of the flesh." In becoming a conscientious father, he stopped by the Commissary every evening after work to buy a Babe Ruth bar for each child to find when he threw his dinner bucket to them as he advanced to kiss his wife. In becoming a conscientious husband he began to accompany his wife to the nightly meetings of her Holy Roller church, and if one of his children playing in the aisle got too noisy while his wife, Sally, was up shouting and looked like she might get the Holy Ghost, he would swat it on the back side.

Then they had a child with a hare lip and Slim became even more involved in their church. His non-member friends wanted him to take the little girl to the doctor, but his church friends and his wife were content for God to heal her. By this time Slim began to pray out loud in the meetings and finally got the Holy Ghost. It was after he had talked in "unknown tongues" that he told the congregation the Lord had told him to handle snakes to show his faith and then the Lord would "make his little girl talk like regular folks."

It was only the year before in another part of the county a child had been bitten by a copper head snake which had gotten loose at a meeting, and the child had died. The state had quickly enacted a law which made it illegal to handle snakes in public. This segment of the Holy-Roller Church had been irate for some time but nothing of a court hearing had occurred.

When Slim Smith made his announcement at the meeting, he said he had already made arrangements to get some rattlesnakes from down in south Georgia and he would have the meeting at his house "so the law can't say nothin' about it."

For several days rumors of this coming event were circulated and many neighbors were skeptical it would be the real thing because snakes were in their holes this time of year in this county.

People had almost quit talking about it when, on a Friday in March, word was spread that Slim had the snakes at home by his kitchen stove and only members of his church could come to his house to a meeting on Saturday night.

When I arrived at Sunday School the next morning, my cousin told me Slim had handled a rattler the evening before and had been bitten. She wanted me to go with her down the street to the store front church where they had brought Slim for the whole church to pray for him.

My cousin's mother taught the class so it was easy to sneak out the door while her mother brushed up on the lesson she would present. We ran down the street and stood with the crowd outside the church for awhile to decide how best to go from there. Soon I saw four high school students perched atop the rear bench. I nodded to my cousin and we crept inside to fill vacant spaces by the high school students.

Poor Slim was squirming in a cane bottomed chair on the stage of the church and his right arm with a black swollen hand was held up by an unknown member of the church. The benches were packed with people who were mumbling in a sing song voice. At irregular intervals an arm would suddenly soar above someone who would yell "hallelujah."

No one was aware of us atop the rear bench, nor apparently of any of the congregation praying for Slim. Finally one woman stood up in the aisle and began talking in unknown tongues but she was totally ignored by everyone seated nearby.

It was obvious that Slim was in severe pain and his sweating face seemed to be turning purple. I wondered if he would die right there and what I should do if he did. He ducked his head down on his arm and wiped the sweat before he turned to face the audience. At this time a member arose and said they would sing Slim's favorite hymn, Will the Circle Be Unbroken In the Land Beyond The Sky. He tried to sing with them but soon gave it up and wiped the tears from his eyes. His elevated hand was at least three times its normal size and was totally black.

The teenagers had gotten bored and were beginning to leave. I felt so uncomfortable about Slim I didn't want to see any more myself, and so I left too.

Slim lived but had much nerve damage in his hand. He could still work in the coal mines but had to learn to eat with his left hand and his wife had to manage all the buttons for him.

During the summer the community had learned that Slim's little hare lipped girl had been taken to a doctor and could now snort out a few understandable words and Slim and Sally were no longer seen at the nightly Holy-Roller meetings.

The fall months in Appalachia are the most spectacular time of year and when Indian Summer occurs, most thoughts are on young adults walking together in the woods and a few industrious parents preparing for winter. It was then an outsider appeared in our midst from Tennessee to inform us that he had heard about Slim Smith and he was here to prove to us that Slim just didn't have enough faith. He would show us. He boasted even louder that he would do it in the church in the middle of town and the law wouldn't bother him.

Peg Leg heard all these comments in town each morning and folks were beginning to ask him what he would do. He always spat a mouthful of tobacco juice before saying a word, and always said, "I'll uphold the law." A few teasers asked if he thought he could get re-elected constable if he broke up the snake handling, and his reply was always "a feller has to do his duty."

It was the following evening after the encircling hues of bronze and gold had been muted into ghostly outlines of serpents, dragons, and vampires, that a basketball game served as the excuse for two friends and me to attend the forbidden meeting.

Aladdin mantles glowed like tiny suns from the lanterns attached by shiny discoid reflectors to the upright skeleton of the building as we made a testy entrance. Observing that a dozen boys with their dates were already perched on the top of the rear bench, we climbed along side them to enjoy a panoramic view of the altar, or stage, or bandstand. At the time of our entrance the proper title for the raised portion at the far end of the church would have been bandstand, for atop each crate was a person with a musical instrument of the most amazing assortment. For a period of time the man with the guitar and one with a mandolin absorbed themselves in peg adjustments while another man made funny faces around a jews harp and looked as though he was flicking hot coals out of his mouth with an index finger.

I spotted Sally Smith on the stage shaking a tambourine and a friend of hers, with an upswept hair-do which added a foot to her height, slithered a set of castanets down the contour of her sheath dress to dreamily enact a scene from a Humphrey Bogart movie. Apparently very little adjustment was required on the tambourine because when someone brought a drum and cymbal set up to the stage and began creaking the screws on the drum, Sally put down her instrument ,picked up her baby lying on the floor and nursed it while chatting with a lady I didn't know.

I wondered what had happened to get Slim and Sally Smith back into the church, and when I asked my friend sitting beside me, she told me the outsider had been by to see Slim several times that week and they had handled the snakes at Slim's house the day before.

Nobody announced the beginning of the meeting, nor did anyone look at a watch to decide it was time to start. It just started when the guitar player gradually changed his plucking, and he began to sing, "I Wandered Far Away From Home." The mandolin player then hit an accentuating chord and joined in picking and nasally twanging the next line, "Where doubts arise and fears dismay." Even after the metallic 4/4 thud of the lever operated cymbal was added, children continued to sit straddle-legged in the aisle rolling a rubber ball to be trapped in a dress tail while another group of children were in the midst of a game of bob jacks. As more harmonizing sounds were added from the unpainted lips of the women in the benches, there was no abatement of extraneous sounds of children squeals, matronly chatter, and male back-slapping as more adults entered the church.

On completion of the first verse of Higher Ground, the guitarist and mandolin player re-tuned while the drummer explored a few rolls on his snare drums before erupting with a rousing fast tempo on the bass drum and began to sing, When The Roll Is Called Up Yonder I'll Be There. A scrubbed faced lady whose long braided hair haloed her head like a coiled snake began to play a previously unnoticed piano, swinging out runs in the treble and syncopating the beat with the bass. An assortment of people in the first three rows of benches beamed happily as they clapped their hands and joined in the singing. Sally Smith returned to the stage to shake the tambourine in time with the treble runs and her friend with the castanets provided a hollow echo to the syncopation. Everyone seemed to be clapping their hands and stomping their feet so loudly that only the drums and piano could be heard above the voices. Intermittently a voice would ring out, "Yeh, Lord" or "Amen", and all the occupants of the front half of the church joined in what looked like a pep rally.

From the front row a freckled, red-faced, withdrawn girl who was a junior in high school and known to all of us on the back bench rose up and faced the congregation with tightly closed eyes. While the hymn was being completed she stood with arms rigidly extended. She was so motionless that her waist length braided pigtails faded their auburn hues into her too matronly brown crepe dress. Was she going to expose us on the back bench for spying on her or was she going to embarrass herself by talking in unknown tongues as had been rumored in school, I wondered as her catatonic stance continued. As I scanned the benches, I could find no other participants who had ever gone as far as high school.

The whooeys, yeh Lord, hallelujahs, and amens had barely quit echoing when she began to speak in a rhythm which resembled Milton's, On His Blindness, "Lord, when I think what a sinner I've been, And with yore bountiful grace and yore ever loving way, I know ye done this so that I may Live with Thee in he'ven."

An overalled miner hitched up his gallowses as he stood and shouted, "Praise be to God. He done it all!"

The high school student then opened her eyes, turned to him and mouthed a smile around the periphery of her wide-spaced decaying teeth, and echoed, "Praise be to God!" She turned another forty-five degrees to face the band stand where Sally Smith sat quietly tapping the cadence of the poem on the tambourine while the castinetted lady with the up-swept hair-do began to croon, "In the land where the night never comes."

A miner had stood up and was giving testimony about a slate fall God had saved him from, and nameless voices from the front of the church appeared to be praying aloud from their seats or kneeling beside them. All the time this was occurring the children's bob jack game continued undisturbed.

As I attempted to hear and observe the ever increasing spontaneous participation of the members singing, praying, gyrating, and testifying in total oblivion to their immediate environment, I felt the cheated frustration of sitting beneath a big top circus trying to simultaneously watch all three performances in the rings beyond.

A blast of cold air hit my shoulders and I turned to see Peg Leg standing in the doorway chewing tobacco. Along side Peg Leg stood the man from Tennessee who had boasted he would handle snakes in public and wouldn't be bitten. He slapped the departing Peg Leg on the back and made his entrance to the front of the church. He carried a Bible but never opened it. Instead he held it up, banged on it to emphasize his words and sounded as though he was preaching a sermon. Every incomplete sentence had a "Praise the Lord" in it but I could get no meaning from his words.

My attention was soon directed to the edge of the altar where an elderly lady knelt while swinging her arms and slapping her hands on the altar as if she were praying in the manner of Moslems. Not far from her a man was undulating in a sensuous manner in the aisle. I decided the outsider had timed his entrance poorly and the meeting would go on with or without him. One could feel a gradually increasing tempo of sound and movement.

For nearly an hour this crescendo continued and even we on-lookers felt a pending climax when suddenly the high school girl jerked herself around to face the rear of the church, and slowly said, "Niena, Niena." She paused as if stunned and began to smile. She seemed to be looking at nothing as she shouted, "Praise the Lord, Niena Niena." Jumping in place, tearing at the tight collar covering her neck, then looking even more wild-eyed and moving as though she needed to escape, she continued shouting, "Niena, Niena."

Somebody propped the door open while more and more people began to talk gibberish or unknown tongues. Then Slim Smith jumped up and yelled, "Whoo-ey! It's a-comin', brother. Glory to God in the highest, I feel it a-comin' on." Then grimacing as if in pain he began to chant, "Zooka booka." I knew the Biblical story of the construction of the tower of Babel being halted by the confusion of unknown tongues and also an item in the book of Corinthians about some missionary work being expedited by the gift of an unknown tongue which was understood by all, but I remained perplexed by the demonstration of faith being exhibited. It was after a small child toddled up to the first row of benches and squatted on the floor to look into the face of a chanting man that all of us on the rear bench top nearly got hysterics.

To keep from giggling I turned to look out the door and Peg Leg was standing there again. He stepped into the door and stood with his hand on the handle of his pistol still in its holster on his hip. Turning again inside, I noticed the church had become quieter and many previous exhibitors were lying on the floor and many children were now stretched out asleep on the benches.

The outsider arose and began to sing Beulah Land but after the second verse he stopped to speak to the congregation, "Now brothers and sisters, you all done seed fer yerself what a good man Slim Smith is. Me and him has been prayin' all week about what the Lord wants us to do. And just tonight when I had the voice of the Holy Spirit, He said fer me and Slim to show these folks jest how much faith we sure enough got. It's time to show we got dominion over the thing He cursed and made to slither on its belly."

Total silence reigned and I became aware that all recent performers were now composed in their seats. "Now I know its against the law to handle snakes, but they ain't no law that's goin' to tell me I can't do what the Lord tells me to do. I'm a law abiding family man and I give Caesar what's a comin' to him, but this here is between the Lord and me and Slim and the Lord."

The lady with the castanet stood and said, "Brother John, I love you like a blood brother, and I know the Lord talks to you all the time. But some of us reckon we can worship the Lord without breaking the law. We all ought to pray mightily about it before we go ahead."

"Sister, you ain't being fair. Think how Brother Slim feels after he tried to show his faith last winter and got bit and then he give up his faith and had his little girl operated on. Now he's been praying and come back to church again and gits the Holy Ghost and needs to know he's got enough faith this time to not git bit."

Some junior high school boys had just entered and this told us the first basketball game was over. Several people in the front of the church turned to see them enter and for some minutes no one seemed to be focused on the issue at hand.

The outsider said, "Folks, we've had a good meeting and I know it's getting late, but we can't leave things up in the air like they are. Why don't you all that want to go, do so, and me and Slim and anybody that wants to stay, can, and we'll pray about it all some more."

"Amen Amen" echoed through the congregation and relieved sighs were heard in abundance. Several people began to don coats and pick up sleeping children and lanterns in preparation for leaving.

My friends and I slipped off the bench and started toward the Good Eats café.

When we entered the Good Eats Café we found Peg Leg propped on a stool at the counter pouring a packet of Stand Back powder into a coke as he talked to the people around him. We hastily crowded into a booth and ordered cokes while we listened to Peg Leg.

"I aint goin' home until all them other people leave the church. They just ain't got worked up enough yet. But mark my word, they'll bring out them snakes before the night's over", Peg Leg was saying.

We had a quick conference in our booth and one of the junior high basketball players who had joined us decided he could run back to the gym to see how the varsity game was going and come back to tell us while we waited for more activity. The other junior high boy who had joined us told us we could know what to do by watching Peg Leg and listening for the noise from the church. So we settled in to sip our cokes and finger initials from the water rings from the coke bottles.

It was at least an hour before Peg Leg flipped the hinge on his peg leg and swallowed the last of his Stand Back before we realized the noise from the church was louder than we had ever heard it. We followed Peg Leg out of the restaurant and ran to the church to take our places atop the rear bench.

I shivered as I became aware of the scene before me. Approximately fifteen men and women were on the stage completely oblivious to everything around them as a rhythmic alto tone swelled up from the gyrating mass. Then one sweating man broke away from the group and went toward the piano and stooped to pick up a vented box.

Suddenly the squeak of Peg Leg's shoe could be heard advancing down the center of the church. When he reached the base of the platform he grasped the handle of his pistol, and in a loud voice said, "I arrest them snakes in the name of the law."

No one moved and not a sound was heard as the man with the box of snakes looked at the people on the stage. Slowly he settled the box on the floor and stood beside it. Peg Leg motioned to a teenager standing nearby and told him and his buddy to go get the snakes and take them to the jail. He then threw the ring of keys to the boy and told them he would follow them down the street so no one would get hurt.

We on the top of the rear bench continued to sit in silence as we watched the people on the stage wilt in tears as the box of snakes was taken away. There were a few curse words welling up from the stage and a few shaking their fists in anger. Most of my friends on the bench followed the teenager to the jail but those of us who weren't supposed to be there anyway, made our way home to tell our parents how the varsity basketball game had gone into overtime but our team had won the game.

Next morning on our way to school we saw all the activity at the city jail. The teenagers were allowed to shoot the snakes and the whole episode faded into oblivion.

Chapter VIII

Washed in the Blood of the Lamb

Each spring in Southern Appalachia, my mother and the other members of the Baptist Missionary Society would begin to prepare food and sleeping arrangements for the coming of the Evangelist and his retinue of singers, accordion players, and once a flutist. If I had asked why this always occurred at this time of year, I would probably have gotten a practical adult answer, such as, it doesn't cost so much to heat the church at night this part of the year, but since I never asked, it was easy to correlate these events with the ebb and flow of the tree sap, or the spring freshening of cows, or it was even possible that they occurred with the peak season of illegitimacy which seemed to always plague our community.

Anticipation of this event left me ambivalent. On the one hand, I dreaded being nagged to complete my evening chores, do my homework, eat supper and be at the church from 7:30 to 9:00 each night, but the other side was that I'd have that time to spend with friends while we giggled, wrote notes, or played tick-tack-toe, while our adult mentors went through their ritual of the revival.

Having been subjected to these ceremonies since the age of four, by the time I reached eight, it was no longer shocking to see grown-ups cry or shout as they hurried to the front of the church to confess vaguely defined sins. The enumerated sins created a tingle of excitement for me, but I wondered how the women felt the next day when they returned to housework and tending too many children, and how the men faced their co-workers with a presumed new leaf turned over in their lives. I tried to find some difference myself, but none was ever apparent in those I saw.

Then Brother Victor arrived with a trembling voice and a smile which did not condescend. His only retinue was a young swarthy complexioned fellow whose collar never wrinkled and whose clear tenor voice, uncharged with tremolos, projected purity and sureness.

The faithful thirty or so church pillars with their captive children were assembled to begin the revival, and we all knew that night would be an exploratory thrust to gain ammunition for the next day's visitations of the recent "back-sliders". The congregation had not dozed into its first catnap with the opening prayer because of its brevity, when we were asked to rise for the "leg stretching" hymn which always preceded a long sermon. We knew something was different when we were told to sing "Love Lifted Me" because that was not a revival hymn, nor even one to precede a sermon entitled Jesus Wept, but there was lusty singing in our soprano variations and energetically holding of the "me" while the few base voices echoed "e-v-e-n me."

On completion of the hymn, Brother Victor thanked the congregation for inviting him to preach while my two friends and I prepared for a long note-passing conversation, but our attention was drawn to center stage again as the handsome young tenor, whose tie and French cuffs belonged on him, began a solo, "Beautiful Garden of Prayer." This was the song my father always quietly sang or hummed as he worked in the garden or helped prepare breakfast, and as I listened admiringly to the singer, he nearly transcended the perfection of my father.

My eyes remained focused on the pulpit and my ribs ignored the elbow jabs of my two friends eager for their notes to be read, but there was still something different about this revival. After Brother Victor repeated his Biblical reference, he went on to explore the reasons people cry. Joy, sorrow, disappointment, and even fear were cited. He made Jesus become a very human person who was fearful of the huge task His father had assigned him. Not once did he evoke shivers in mentioning the everlasting fire which had always been a major part of the revival formula. We didn't even have to hear about poor Job whom God had abused repeatedly just to prove a point.

The "Invitational Hymn" after the sermon would surely follow the pattern I knew so well. After all, Brother Victor had a trembling voice to make everyone in the church cry, I thought cynically, as the pianist struck the opening chords of "Just As I Am." Before the first verse was over, most of the women had removed a white lawn handkerchief from inside a puffed sleeve and had sponged the corners of their eyes. Abruptly, the evangelist stood on tip-toe and stopped the hymn to announce, "Will all you staunch members of this church who want to thank God for your gift of faith and desire to show your fellow man that you want to try harder to lead a Christian life, please come forward?" As each adult responded and went forward with dignity, they shook hands with the Evangelist, then the tenor, and finally with each other, until the space between the front pew and the pulpit became a mass of smiling faces and shaking hands. Confounded by the lack of sadness and bored by the continuous handshaking, it had not occurred to those of us in the rear third of the church that we had just been singled out for concentrated evangelistic attention, so we joined in the benedictory drone, "the Lord keep me and thee while we are absent one from the other."

It was good to talk to Jesus that night from the security of my bed, for now the want list I would present to Him seemed less selfish in His newly comprehended humanness, and it was the first revival night I had not been tormented by a nightmare of being on a smoldering ledge in a cave consumed with lapping tongues of flame in the eternal hell.

The next night we were eager to hear the tenor sing but didn't expect a drastic change in the approach of the Revivalist.   W   e were, however, soon made aware that Brother Victor liked to attack indirectly because his theme didn't sound like a revival topic and his opening prayer was a brief thanks for the growing congregation and a plea for God to give him the appropriate words to fill our hearts. There were now enough pews filled that passing the collection plate was worthwhile as the tenor exhibited his skill singing "The Lord's Prayer", and we sighed admiringly.

Soon it became apparent that Brother Victor wasn't talking to children this evening for love to a pre-adolescent girl is an unexpected nickel for an ice cream cone, or a new pair of shoes, and love of fellow-man is an obligation which makes people be polite to each other. In due time, we took up paper for tick-tack-toe and began to play. I'd kept an intermittent ear toward the pulpit so when the evangelist re-read the text from Corinthians which ended, "the greatest of these is charity" didn't cause me to be surprised. He paused dramatically, folded his arms on the pulpit and leaned forward confidentially, and said, "God has told me that bad, black, evil blood flows in the veins of some of you tonight. He has told me that every one of you who has openly made bad remarks about his fellow-man is carrying the burden within his heart of other equally grave sins. Your conscience plagues you to erase these thoughts with drink and compound the errors of your ways. Some of you know you don't have much longer to live, and you cry in secret because you know you won't be joining your beloved mother in God's mansion in the sky." Again he paused, but the spell was broken by honks from male blown noses and female sniffs. He continued: "To err is human and as we admit our secret sins to ourselves, we admit the humanness of the sins of others. Even those in which we were wronged." Rising to a trembling crescendo he added, "But the most divine of all human attributes is to forgive!" He raised a beseeching hand above his lifted head and closed his eyes to pray, "Dear Heavenly Father, You have brought these suffering tortured souls here tonight to hear Thy word. You have made me the simple lamp to show them the light. Now give them the courage to come forward to ask Thy forgiveness and forgiveness of their fellow-man. Bolster their courage with the realization of the peace they will enjoy for the rest of their lives and into eternity. Amen."

Promptly, the pianist and the choir, led by our new Adonis began to sing "Almost Persuaded." The congregation rose stiffly to its feet but only lips and adam's apples moved through the entire first verse. The room remained electric and the evangelist remained in a mute catatonic stance with his arm and head uplifted and his eyes closed. We were into the third verse of "Almost Persuaded" when a shuffle was heard and old Judge Small was seen "scissor-gating" toward the front of the church. The further he advanced, the fewer choir voices were heard until only the tenor finished the verse "almost but lost." Judge Small turned to face the congregation, dried his eyes, and began, "I reckon there ain't never been a bigger sinner in the whole world than me. I reckon they ain't many of you here tonight and heaps that ain't here, that I ain't done something against. I know it's a heap to ask, but, somehow its more important for you-all to forgive me than for God to, 'cause He forgave Nicodemus I seem to recollect", and he lowered his head and began to cry again, while the congregation stood awkwardly and looked at nothing.

A new stir caught everyone's attention. Mr. Hartman, a stately, red-faced, rotund gentleman in his fifties was hurrying to the front of the church with right hand extended, as he said, "You said you wanted everybody's forgiveness and I guess that means me too." Pandemonium occurred when the brief handshake was followed by Mr. Hartman stooping to receive the tearful embrace of the once fornicating crooked old judge. Finally order was restored by Brother Victor who preceded his benediction with the triumphant announcement that this was a major victory for the Lord, but the unstated fact was that twelve more nights remained to capture the adolescents and alcoholics, for the quality of this night's take would insure a packed house throughout the extent of the revival.

The memory of that night's service obliterated my "want list" to Jesus when I went to bed because I wondered if any change would be noticeable in Judge Small and Mr. Hartman the next day. What did one really feel when he got "saved" and had total faith in God? Do you just quit thinking evil and quit hating people? Do people in "grace" dread doing their Christian duty and does faith keep you from worrying about what people think of you?

On my way to school next morning, I saw Mr. Hartman taking down his beer sign while his wife and asthmatic son washed off the funeral parlor plaque to restore the family to its original role in the community. Simultaneously, Judge Small was prodding his step son to clean the lobby of the City Hall, as he rumbled on about having a clean honest court from now on.

The next night the church was so full it looked like the time when my slain "Union Organizing" uncle was there in his casket for his funeral. The sermons continued to be about love, kindness, mercy, and the gift of Roosevelt to end the Depression. Was it any wonder that on the fifth night, which had the theme, "Whatsoever a man sows, that shall he also reap", Brother Victor convinced my sister and me, as well as most of the pre-adolescents there, that it was sheer joy to lead a never ending life of goodness. We all went sobbing to the front of the church, and as near as I could discern we cried because we were ashamed to be seen. Beneath this hope for a new feeling and a changed me lay the years of fire and brimstone, so that if the new me proved to be a disappointment, this act of humility was a small price to pay to avoid the thing I feared most--fire.

I half expected my mother to come up and jerk me away and tell me I didn't belong there with the older children, but she didn't even come to offer me a damp hand nor a hug. The "Invitational" hymn had been sung fifteen times and the congregation had been milked of every guilt ridden child in attendance. Even during the mile walk home, neither parent said a word to me.

Jesus and I were estranged when I got into bed that night because I didn't feel any different, but as sleep finally came I was still hopeful the morning would find a new me full of confidence and dignity. Instead, the morning brought a hushed conversation with my mother while I dried the breakfast dishes.

Maybe if Mother hadn't used the same hushed tone of voice as she had used two years before when she had told me about how women split open and God let the baby out, I might not have gotten so confused. When she asked me if I really understood about God, I tried to say what I thought she wanted to hear and said, "Yes, I love God and His son, Jesus, and I will try harder to always be good. Now I won't think bad thoughts and I'll quit sneaking away to go play with Little Eileen." For the first time I could remember I was told to go play rather than being given a list of chores to complete, so I added, "Is it all right for Christians to play? Shouldn't I go start reading the Bible?"

That evening Mother took me to see Brother Victor. He asked me numerous questions to which I gave Biblical quotations and references, much as I would have used in a Bible Sword Drill in Vacation Bible School. Finally I heard him scold Mother for questioning my maturity and love of God, and I floated out of that room a new me.

Christianity brought a close to our revival note passing and tick-tack-toe games, and the very next day, my friends and I realized the thwarting nature of our new selves. We had found a penny but now it would be gambling and sinful to spend it on a punch board to try to win a nickel candy bar we could all enjoy. One friend thought it was just as sinful to want to spend it on a punch board as to do it, and the other friend asked what else a penny could be used for, so we did it. When we didn't win the candy bar we blamed it on God. We discussed at length whether or not we'd want to do sinful things after we got baptized Then came a story of a Holiness preacher and a man he was baptizing in the river being drowned. I reminded my friends the church baptistery would be used for our rite and we didn't have to worry about it.

Before the evening of the planned baptism on Saturday night, the roster of candidates for baptism had swelled to one-hundred-fifty (150) souls, a gross success in any evangelistic parlance. The church pastor had decided my sister and I should be baptized simultaneously, thus adding to my mother's delight.

Saturday morning was usual in its demand for early completion of our weekly chores, but the unusual command was for us to find all the safety pins we owned. Failing to satisfy my mother's demand, we were sent to the store to buy two additional cards of pins. Finally we were informed it was time to dress in our Sunday tan pongee dresses, white ribbed stockings, and patent leather shoes. Additional clothes and towels were placed in a paper poke to take to the church.

An hour before the service was to begin about fifty of us and our mothers were herded into an unheated Sunday School room to be prepared for baptism. I soon became astounded at the preparations made. First, a mother lifted the a daughter's dress and slip to pin her bloomers front, back, and sides to the hem of her overlying clothes. Next, her stockings were secured in three places to her slip. Finally, about six pins were used to attach slip and dress front to back from crotch to knees. It was now impossible to sit, so we stood red-faced, feeling diapered and restrained, and all for presumed modesty. We remained silent, shackled and stiff legged, while we watched the baptism of the two town heroes, Mr. Hartman and Judge Small.

Now it was time for my sister and me to waddle awkwardly to the baptistery and just as we attained view of the audience, the cold, cold water penetrated our shoes. Thoughts of a loving Jesus and eternal life have never been my response to cold, but immobilized with safety pins there was no running away. The pastor was now climbing the steps toward us and talked of "suffer little children to come unto me." His little children were suffering all right as the cold water inched higher and at waist height I was breathless. Then a safety pin came undone and jabbed me in the thigh so I let go of the pastor's arm which I had just been instructed to hold with one hand and my nose with the other. While he held my sister's back and nose with his hand, I heard "I baptize thee in the name of the Father," but the remainder must have been part of my struggle.

"Dipped in the valley of the shadow of death," I thought as I heard the congregation chuckle. Then we were escorted back to the cold Sunday School room to drip dry until we could gain access to the towels.

Still determined to find a new me, I went exhausted to bed that night and returned to the Jesus of my memory. I abandoned the flowery thee's, thy's, and thou's. Instead I said, "Please, Jesus, help me to be good and sure, and let people say nice things about me and not laugh at me."

For years, modifications of this prayer recurred, until finally in adult life I was able to talk to myself instead of Jesus, and say, "I can strive for perfection because it pleases me and not because I need to tally points for God. And, as for worrying about what people think of me, people are too occupied with what people think of themselves to be concerned about the impression I make."

Chapter IX

Jesus Loves the Little Children

There were few dull moments in the hollow in which I grew up after I reached age six and started to school. In addition to the assigned chores I had at home, I had a calf or cow to see to and my father had given me a half acre garden plot to tend and gather the vegetables. I sold the vegetables we didn't consume and made enough money to buy the material for my clothes, shoes, and school supplies. And even though my mother didn't approve of me playing with most of the children near my age who lived near us, I still managed to see several of them on the sly.

It was in early summer on this occasion when I had slipped away from home and met Little Eileen at the spout. She told me I should find some shoes that needed fixing so I could go with her to the shoe shop so we could see the baby in the jar the shoe shop man's daughter had found that day in the creek. I had a quarter which would pay for new heels on my school shoes, so I told her I would meet her back at the spout in a half hour and we would go to town.

My mother didn't know about the baby in the jar when I told her I had the quarter to pay for new heels for my school shoes so she agreed for me to take the shoes into town.

Little Eileen and I ran most of the way to town and when we arrived, we found a line of people extending from the shoe shop a full half block to the post office. Each person in the line had at least one pair of shoes in hand and there was a lively conversation evident among all the people waiting.

We went to the foot of the line and didn't say a word because we wanted to hear what was being said by the group of middle aged women just ahead of us. I heard one say, "That flash flood we had yesterday must have washed it all the way down to town from up in Hooter Hollow." Another woman in the group began to give names of girls and count on her fingers. Finally I began to realize she was giving the names of teenagers and unmarried adult women who lived in Hooter Hollow where I lived.

Then they seemed to get into an argument and another woman declared, "I know it couldn't have been little Missy because her daddy won't let her even go to Sunday School by herself." As the line advanced toward the shoe shop, we heard many more names mentioned, and I whispered to Little Eileen that I wondered if they would mention any members of our families. Before we arrived at the shoe shop, they had narrowed the list down to a teenage girl who lived near us, and they decided it must have been her because her father sold moonshine and ran a card game in his kitchen while he wife was out earning money doing housework.

When we entered the shoe shop, the fetus in a mason jar was on the counter just beyond the cash register where the horde of people were standing with shoes to be repaired. Each got a paper receipt and advanced on to the point where he or she could get a good look at the specimen. The invariable comment was, "Look, it was a little boy."

I got a good look at the fetus which looked just like the pictures I'd seen in the Book of Knowledge I wasn't supposed to read. It was in a quart Mason jar in a clear liquid and the umbilical cord was still attached. Sure enough there was a little penis protruding from its front even though the fetus was slightly folded as if it were quietly asleep. The ribs showed plainly but the head looked too big to me. Little Eileen and I made no comments as we looked at it and left the shoe shop.

We didn't have much to say to each other on our walk back to the spout, but once there, we sat down to discuss it in detail. We wondered if it had been an ordinary miscarriage because it wasn't normal, or could it have been the result of someone using slippery elm. Neither of us knew enough about pregnancy to voice an opinion, so we decided the best thing to do was to discuss it with Little Eileen's mother when we could find her alone. When I got home I started my evening chores so as to have more think time and to plan how I could snitch The Book of Knowledge out of the book case to have another look at the unborn baby I had seen there before.

I managed to accomplish retrieving the book before supper time and hid it in my room so I could read it after everyone had gone to bed. Nothing was mentioned of my trip to town and we had a normal evening except that I announced I was sleepy just as soon as the nightly Amos and Andy program on the radio was finished. Once in my room, I placed a blanket at the base of the door so my parents couldn't see my light was still on. For over an hour I sat in my pajamas on the side of the bed and read every word of the chapter on fetal development. I concluded the baby I had seen in the Mason jar was less than four months in its development and the head was supposed to be bigger in proportion to the body. But there was nothing to tell me whether it was a miscarriage or abortion. Abortion was a new word for me and there was no way my eight year old mind could decide how that was carried out, so I went to sleep and decided Little Eileen's mother would have to answer the remainder of my questions.

The shoe shop man's business flourished for about two more weeks until the local doctor returned from vacation and learned of the specimen on display at the shoe shop. He angrily went to retrieve his specimen, and the whole community returned to normal on learning the fetus had been thrown out by the doctor's substitute when he was cleaning up the office. The whole event became so uninteresting that Little Eileen and I never asked her mother about abortions.

The local doctor didn't take another vacation for five years and then he left for good. He quietly took all the debris from his office up to Graveyard Hill when he was preparing to leave and nobody bothered to look through it all. It must have been at least three months later that a group of eight to ten year old boys were leveling a pile of junk so they would have a place to spin tops. In the bottom of the pile there was a Mason jar with a tiny baby in it. One boy thought they must have been digging in a grave and immediately began to cry. The others began to laugh at him, so he ran home to his grandmother, and told all.

The grandmother was upset too and decided the safest thing to do was to "call the law." Promptly, she awoke her husband and sent him to town to tell Peg Leg, the Constable, what had occurred.

Peg Leg spent about an hour finding twelve men loafing around the post office. They were to be members of an inquest. They all climbed up to Graveyard Hill to see first hand what all the commotion was about. After they looked at the fetus in the Mason jar, one of the members of the inquest remembered the episode of the specimen on display in the shoe shop. Then others remembered too. Without further ado, they decided it was the same baby in the bottle, so Peg Leg made the hole a little bigger and buried the specimen.

As I got older and more reflective in my thinking, I decided I had learned a lot in my little Appalachian hollow, and should not feel disadvantaged for having come from the mountains.

Chapter X

God Will Take Care of You

Halloween was not a Trick or Treat night in Appalachia before World War II. Instead, it was a night to be feared and dreaded because it was a night of mischief and destruction. The limits were confined to the imagination of the pre-adolescent and teenage boys. The worst deed of the few teenage girls who were allowed out on Halloween night was to smear soap on the windows of cars and display windows of the merchants in town. Out-houses were turned over, tin cans were attached to the tails of any cat which could be caught, and the ends of foot bridges were whacked off so the next person attempting to get across a stream was made to slide into the cold water of the creek or river.

The school principal and elders of the churches got together and decided we should have a carnival at the school gym so the youngsters would be occupied and not spend the night being destructive. Together, the community got a bushel of apples and tubs of water to dip them in, water pistols to be used for a booth for target practice, bingo games were put together, and a display of colas and ham sandwiches was apparent when one entered the gym. There was even a primitive juke box in an area of the basketball court which was marked off so young couples could dance.

While this event didn't prevent all out-houses from being overturned, nor soap smeared around town, it was well attended, and reduced the degree and quantity of destruction. Even the oldsters seemed to enjoy wearing a mask and eerie clothes to this affair.

It was the third year of the Halloween carnival when our catastrophe occurred. The gym was full of people and the juke box was playing when my father happened to go to the door of the gym to get some fresh air. He happened to look over the mountain and saw a bright glow from the hollow in which we lived. Hurriedly, he gathered my siblings, mother, and me, and told us to get in the car. There was no explanation of why we were going home, but he was driving faster than I had known him to ever go so there was no mistake it was a crisis.

As we turned up Hooter Hollow, we could see a building on fire and I knew it was our house. However, as we got closer, it proved to be our barn.

I had milked and fed my cow early that evening, but I couldn't remember if I had turned her out into the pasture or left her feeding in the barn. I began to cry. Dad promptly ordered, "Now hush! That won't help a bit."

When we came to a halt on the road in front of our property, I ran around the barn and out to the pasture, and breathed a big sigh of relief when I saw my Daisy,a jersey cow, standing there chewing her cud.

In my absence, my father and four other men had found a long log and were pushing it against the back wall of the burning barn to make it fall toward the road. The women nearby told me that was to prevent the barn from catching our house on fire. Now there was nothing to do but stand there and watch the barn, hay, farm tools, and a spare tire burn to the ground.

One of our neighbors even brought a bucket of milk and some sandwiches to the road and we squatted on stones and ate while the red glow gradually waned. At the very end, someone hooked up a hose to our pump on the front porch so the embers could be killed and no one would have to worry about a wind coming up in the night and the fire spreading.

When I finally got in bed, I said a long silent prayer and thanked God for taking such good care of us and Daisy.

I wasn't very perceptive that night, but my father and many of the neighbors were. Everyone who lived in Hooter Hollow was there except the teenage son of a neighbor who lived two houses from us. But this boy, even though five years older than me, was a good friend who seemed to enjoy playing with me and would go to the woods with me to cut down saplings which we made into stilts. I knew he wasn't very smart and he seemed able to read only comic books which he always carried in the hip pocket of his overalls.

While we were eating breakfast next morning my friend's father knocked on our door, and as soon as he had lit a cigarette, cleared his throat he said, "I hate to have to tell you this, but it was my boy who set your barn on fire. I've already give him a whippin' like he ain't never had before, but that don't do you no good. As you know, I'm out of work, but I'm a good carpenter. I can't afford to buy the lumber, but I'll build your barn back, 'cause I'm responsible." It took very little time for Dad to agree to buy enough lumber for him to get started and his son could help him after school and on Saturdays, but his son was to stay away from our house and always act like a gentleman.

On our way to school that morning my sister whispered to me that she had heard the reason Jay, the boy who had burned our barn, was not very smart was that some men had caught him having sex with a cow. She explained to me the reason Mother always fussed when I had been in the woods with him was because she was afraid he might try to do something with me. I replied that he had always been a normal boy to me and he always helped me when his super strength would help. By this time there were lots of our classmates around us saying how sorry they were about our fire, so nothing further was said about Jay.

Jay dropped out of school that winter and worked with his father on our barn until it was finished in record time. It really was a better barn and attached garage than we had before so we only had to buy new plow handles, a corn sheller, new ropes, and hoes. The new barn even had a hay rack and feed bin in the cow stall, so all was well.

We didn't see much of Jay after the barn was rebuilt and then World War II came into our lives. Jay couldn't be drafted because of his inability to learn, but eventually he went to Cincinnati with an older brother and got a job in a defense factory.

I was home from college one Christmas and saw Jay driving a car past our house. I asked my mother about him and learned he seemed to be normal now and acted like any young man would. She told me he even sent a part of his pay check home each pay period to help out his elderly parents.

The remainder of this story is hearsay because I was working away from home or in school when Jay returned home after World War II was over and the factory in which he worked was closed. He had a used car, wife, and three children. His wife was a city girl and not many people around home liked her because she talked too much and was never happy with anything Jay or the children did.

Jay tried to work in a coal mine but was soon fired. He then got a job delivering furniture for a store in the county seat. That lasted about three months, and then he had to be content with being a bag boy in a grocery, but he seemed to make enough money that they could take a long car ride every Sunday afternoon. His three children had fitted into the neighborhood with no difficulty and two were in school.

Everybody in town knew them because Jay's wife spent a lot of time at the ice cream parlor in town. Most tried to avoid her because she had nothing to talk about except all the things Jay and the children did wrong.

Both of Jay's parents died so Jay and his family moved into their house and his many brothers and sisters still lived in the cities to which they had migrated during the war.

Suddenly and unexpectedly, one Sunday just before sun down, a state highway patrol car pulled up in front of the ice cream parlor in town. Jay's wife and the three children got out of the car and went into the ice cream parlor. The children were silent and his wife was wiping tears from her face. The highway patrolman entered the parlor and bought a coke. While he was drinking the coke, the proprietor struck up a conversation with him to learn what had happened. The story the patrolman told was eerie. It seems they were driving across Tan Yard Hill when Jay stopped the car. He told his wife and the children to get out of the car. His wife began to argue with him and asked why they were to get out of the car. Jay calmly told them he was tired of her always complaining about him, and he had decided to cure her problem for her. Once the car doors were closed, Jay speeded up the car and drove it over the mountain. When people in passing cars stopped to see what had happened, and climbed down the mountain to where Jay and the car were located, he was dead with a smile on his face.

Right after the funeral, Jay's wife and children sold his parent's house and had enough money to go back to the city from which they had come. They were never heard from again.

Chapter XI

Rock of Ages

My first awareness of Atee was after she was already of bifocal age. Satan himself could not have told a fib to her as she stared in disbelief with her head tilted down to see through the long range half of her gold rimmed bifocals. If I concentrated vigorously enough before I wilted from her stare some relief was to be afforded in looking down her Roman nose to study her dentured over-bite, and a chinless turkey waddle which shook with each raspy breath.

Atee's only mode of conversation was in the form of a question, and these were uttered in such rapid sequence there would be six unanswered before one became aware of not having been allowed time enough to answer the first one. By this time she would emit an accusing query, "Don't you love your Atee any more? Don't you appreciate all she does for you?"

My answer was invariably, "Yes, Atee, I love you and thank you for all you do for me." Then I'd kiss her on her bearded cheek. These encounters were usually when she would be fitting a dress or skirt, and they were made even more uncomfortable by my having to stand leaning backward at a sixty degree angle so she could reach my apparel over her protruding abdomen.

I always looked like I'd just stepped away from Little Orphan Annie's clothes line because every dress was a shirt waist with a belt of the same material, and a four gored skirt. Mother always agreed with her to keep the pattern the same because changing the style would be wasteful and, according to Atee, "Waste is a sin." I got the impression that waste was a more carnal sin than gluttony. I wondered why the sin of gluttony was only mentioned if she were talking about alcohol or green apples. Waste was such a sin to Atee that when she stayed for dinner she would sit with an empty plate until I had finished mine and after giving me another lecture on waste, she would proceed to make a rapid meal of my leavings.

That Atee had always occupied a dominant role in our household became even more apparent when I became aware of the peculiar arrangement of our house. It seems that Atee moved into their temporary house with them when my parents returned from their honeymoon. There was no such thing as an architect in Appalachia, so my parents drew up the plans and gave them to the builder and they set to work. But, each morning as Atee was en route to school, she would inspect what the builders had done and change the plans to suit her fancy. I suppose they were as afraid of her tongue as I, because the kitchen was in the front of the house two rooms and a hallway away from the dining room. The bath room was next to the kitchen but there was no running water, and a water bucket was kept on a board atop the small end of the tub. Hot water for our Saturday baths was obtained from the reservoir on the kitchen stove and water for flushing had to be pumped from the well beneath the front porch.

There were no wall electric sockets because the children they would have might get electrocuted with them, and all the bare bulbs suspended from the ceiling were long enough to be changed without the use of a ladder because ladders were dangerous.

When I asked my Father why he had always put up with her, he replied in his soft mellow manner, "I kept thinking she would get married or move out of the country." Finally he did criticize her, and it changed the lives of all of us to some degree.

My Father brought his sixty year old recently widowed cousin home from church for Sunday dinner and introduced his cousin to Atee who was forty. Promptly she left the room and did not return until after the cousin had departed, and it was then that Dad told her how rude she had been. She wrote a letter of apology to the cousin so he returned for dinner the following Sunday. Six weeks later, when I was two years old, our Warm Morning heater in our living room became the backdrop for their wedding. Since my new Uncle Em had been a frugal, hard-working man with much property, they enjoyed a prolonged wedding trip, and we enjoyed our new found freedom.

I never knew which of them had selected the site of the house they built on their return from the cities of the mid-west, but the treeless hillside two hundred feet above an unbanked C curve in the highway was surely too steep for a crop of corn. But it is possible they put their house in that location because their favorite past time, other than Atee's Bible and dictionary reading, was to sit on their front porch and watch the bloody remains of cars which could not negotiate the curve and crashed into the Cumberland River.

Throughout the period of Atee's domestic tranquility, sin and religion were never mentioned, nor did they attend church. There was even a note of affection as she called him Mr. H., whether to him or others. Apparently the sun ceased to shine when she bluntly told him he needed to bathe and change clothes more frequently. His reply to this was to tell her he was content and if she wanted it different she would have to do it. Henceforth she bathed and dressed him. This acquiescence, however, was avenged with Uncle Em giving each of his seven daughters two thousand dollars and Atee only one thousand. Also, by this time the rumor that she had only married him for his money had gotten back to Atee. She sought consolation from my parents and she went back to church. They drifted on silently for about two more years, and they always shared the household expenses and even divided the butter and egg money. Atee put her savings into preferred stocks and savings bonds, and Uncle Em kept his in his socks until the wad required him to take it to the bank.

For several years I thought Atee's domination of me was because I was the daughter she couldn't have. I couldn't escape her possession of me because each time she came to visit she would relate that she had named me and had paid hard cash to do so. She had bought one hundred dollars of preferred Kentucky Utilities stock in my name and each time she reminded me of it she added, "If I'd bought common stock that would have been gambling, but preferred stock pays the same amount every three months and that's just like having a savings account, only better." Except through part of the depression, a check for $2.38 arrived in the mail quarterly and provided the stimulus for many hours of my poring over the Sears, Roebuck catalogue as well as a few trips to the penny candy counter. Finally I learned she had also bought an equal amount of stock for my sister and twice that amount for my brother so I never could decide why she felt I was so beholden to her.

Each Thursday morning, until I started to school, our morning routine changed to accommodate Atee's arrival at nine a.m. Instead of an hour of writing with my wrong hand I swept the kitchen, washed my face and combed my hair all by myself while Mother washed the dishes and put the beans on the stove to simmer. Then Atee would appear carrying a large black purse, a peck size basket under her arm and an umbrella. Her kisses were always moist and her bearded face pricked, but worst of all was that I had to become a contortionist to get beyond her over-hanging tummy to hug her. Then she would retrieve from her basket whatever gift she had brought Mother and me, be it apple, tomato, or a partially finished garment for me to try on. On acceptance of a gift, I must not only thank her but hug and kiss her again, all before she asked me if I loved her, and, if so, how much.

Atee once recited a poem about idle hands and evil thoughts and if those two phenomena are related, she lived the most sanctimonious life imaginable. She not only kept her hands busy with sewing, needle work, or peeling fruit for canning, but she also kept me busy too. Before I was six she had already taught me to hook and braid rugs, embroider napkins, run a pedal sewing machine, and crochet, but she gave up on teaching me to knit with my left hand.

I had already started school before we had a reprieve from Atee's weekly visits--Uncle Em got a belly ache and refused treatment for eight days. Then for three weeks after surgery for a ruptured appendix and peritonitis, Uncle Em hovered on the brink of eternity, while Atee hovered over the private duty nurses who attended him. As his recuperation progressed so did his guilt. His first act on his return home was to empty his sock to Atee and equal for her the amount he had previously bestowed on each of his daughters. Again it looked as though they would live happily ever after, while we and the church would enjoy our unmanaged affairs.

The only exception to this respite was that I was required to spend two weeks with them each summer. My "vacation" was always at the time when their beans, corn, tomatoes, and pepper were ready to be harvested and the excess frying chickens needed to be sold.

Each dawn, after a defiant flush of the toilet, and a splash of hot water on my face, I downed a hearty breakfast while I watched in wonder how Atee could chew so rapidly in the front of her stark white store bought teeth. After drying the dishes washed in three day old dish water, I accompanied Atee up to the chicken lot to catch the eight fryers she wanted me to sell that day.

Their legs were tied together and they were placed under a galvanized tub to prevent escape before I was given two baskets and a lard can to take to the dew wet garden to pick the vegetables I was to peddle that day. My itchy legs from the wet leaves and occasional "pack-saddle sting" spurred me to get it done in a hurry. By this time, Uncle Em would have had his breakfast and was ready to help me organize my load, as well as tell me how much to charge for each item.

My usual load consisted of four chickens hanging from each shoulder, two gallon buckets of beans or peas in one hand, and a peck size basket of onion, corn, peppers, or carrots in the other hand. If I were lucky, a roadside café about a mile away would have enough interested coffee drinkers to take half of my heavy awkward load. If not, I had to maneuver across a swinging bridge and walk another half mile to get to a mining town of mud roads and grassless yards. Sometimes a housewife would untie two fryers from my shoulder, jostle them for weight, feel under their wings, and ask how much. I'd have been happy to give both away to her except for remembering the vitriolic tongue of Atee, so that when the potential buyer would begin to bargain, I would blush while tying the fryer back in place and walk on.

There were times I thought the buyer responded to the pity she felt for me and my load. Usually I could sell everything in time to traverse the three miles back across the swinging bridge and get to Atee;s house in time for lunch, and be given my reward of a dime for the five or six dollars I'd collected. Every other day after lunch I was "allowed to make more money" by catching and burning bean bugs at the rate of one hundred bugs for a penny. Each time accompanying my reward was a lecture, "From little grains of sand mighty oceans grow. You must learn to resist temptation and save your money because you never know when disaster will strike." My real reward was being allowed to go to the river all by myself to fish or swim, or collect mussel shells, if the river wasn't up or muddy or if it might not rain. It was during this time I would count the days until it would all be over, and try to figure out why my parents wanted me to be there in the first place.

There appeared always to be an inverse relationship between Atee's religious fervor and domestic tranquility. It was impossible for me, a niece, to imagine the role in bed of this rigid, always positive, righteous, self-professed paragon of virtue whose avowed purpose in life was to love and sacrifice for me so that my "light might shine for the glory of God" It was during one of my two week "vacations" at her home that her religious zeal rose to its zenith and led her to build a church.

Each night, flashlight in hand, Atee, Uncle Em, and I walked two miles to a revival being held by an unknown evangelist who was in the region selling seeds anyway. The first week was like every revival I'd attended, but at the Sunday morning service, the regular preacher took over. He stumbled through the Bible text in which Jesus washed the feet of Mary Magdalene, and brought out a number three galvanized tub half full of cold water. The first victim of this ritual of humility was an aged, hard of hearing, disheveled man sitting with his ear trumpet on the seat beside him. The preacher unlaced the brogans of the old man and rolled up his clean overall legs, found he had an extra step to do to unpin the socks from his flannel long legged underwear before the stench of the old man's long neglected feet hit the preacher's sense of smell. All was quiet for a few minutes but when the preacher doused the odor with a big splash, the old man recoiled in shock. He pulled his feet out of the water and yelled, "Ain't ye goin' to dry 'um?'"

The preacher pulled a white handkerchief out of his hip pocket and made it black from rubbing the old man's feet, while he talked about cleanliness being next to Godliness.

I thought he should have wiped the tobacco stain from the old man's grey beard, but I could begin to hear a whisper in the benches while a line of faithful formed to have their feet washed in the now very dirty water. Suddenly Atee grabbed my arm and said "Let's go!" Her exit was no less grand than the Triumphant Entry in Aida, except there were no silver toned horns. All her friends and Uncle Em were with her so only the click of high heels and steel taps could be heard in the aisle. I was still trying to take it all in and looking back in the church when she firmly stated, "The very idea of a foot washing Baptist coming here. Why, it's a caution!"

Atee led us all to an abandoned store where there were still a few orange crates and cracker barrels. Hastily the women blew the dust off the containers so as not to soil their Sunday clothes when they sat on the containers.

The seed man evangelist had just come in and raised his arms to lead us in prayer before he even looked for a seat. Then, Attee, with the deftness of Alban Barkley, didn't even get to her feet to announce they would form a new church that would be called Riverside Missionary Baptist Church and the seed man would be the pastor. The next item of business was his salary which included free room and board at her house when he was in town and enough butter, eggs, milk and vegetables to maintain him and his wife when he was at home.

Uncle Em, ordinarily a very silent man, became vocal enough to donate land and lumber to build the church. It wasn't going to be convenient to any of them except Atee and Uncle Em, but without a dissenting voice, it was agreed.

Atee got to her feet to state the next edict, "Now we have to show those foot-washers we mean business, and since Brother Nathan will still be with us for another week, we ought to have our own revival right here." Amen echoed through the attendees to the bare walls. "We need to build benches and a pulpit, and if you men will take care of that I'll go to the book store first thing in the morning to get song books and a Bible."

The industrious congregation of twenty had a peacock strut as they gathered at dusk in the lantern lit store church the following night. All were seated on the unsanded four board benches while Brother Nathan tearfully extolled the miracles of God when people gathered for the work of His cause. Someone had donated a pump organ even though there was no one to play it, but Brother Nathan was sure that someone would come forward to lead the way.

There was only one adult non-member in the building and she was a well known "sportin' lady". Any time the good ladies of the community got together for an "Aint it Awful" conversation, the quality and quantity of Miz Jessie's after dark activities were discussed. She was rumored to bootleg "white lightning", run a card game in her kitchen, and a five year old daughter proved that at least once she had been sinfully indiscrete.

Brother Nathan began his sermon with the story of the return of the prodigal son. Frequent amens from the small congregation seemed to spur him on. By the time he got to the end of his preaching, his voice had attained a tremulous character. He began to sing "Almost Persuaded" and the congregation rose and joined in the hymn.

Suddenly, up jumped Miz Jessie who yelled, "Oh Lord, firgive me of my many sins! Preacher, will Jesus really take a woman that's been as bad as me?"

From out of the congregation someone shouted, "Praise the Lord!" Brother Nathan started down the aisle toward Miz Jessie, and as she came forward to meet him he hugged her and accompanied her to the front of the church where she knelt and joined the rest of the people in crying.

Atee's timing was perfect. She produced tears with the others but when time came to restore order, her tears disappeared without wiping, and her face bore no mark of an earlier display of emotion. She promptly appointed herself church secretary-treasurer, and announced Miz Jessie's name and address (the first I'd known her house had a number instead of being the cat house on the hill); then she asked for a voice vote to give her membership in the church.

Atee continued her manipulation of the situation saying, "Now we all know the best way to keep a member from falling from grace is to get him or her busy working for the Lord. We've named ourselves Missionary Baptist Church so we need a mission and somebody to run it, and Miz Jessie needs a job so she can legitimately support her little daughter and not be forced back to the ways of sin." Everyone agreed and in due course, Miss Jessie was installed in a hut on the back side of the mountain to minister to five families, of which four were already "snake handling Holy-Rollers".

I saw a lot of Brother Nathan and Miz Jessie that week. Brother Nathan moved in with us and I was assigned to sleep on the living room sofa. Miz Jessie visited potential members for the church in the morning and came to Atee's in mid afternoon. I'd pour us all a cold glass of grape juice when everybody was collected on the front porch and then help Atee with fixing supper. After we ate it was time to go to church again, and by this time I was yearning for sleep.

An incident happened on Thursday which led me to question the validity of Miz Jessie's conversion, but I couldn't tell it without incriminating myself. I had pilfered thirty-five cents from the sale of Atee's fryers and vegetables, and had it tied in the corner of my handkerchief. When Miz Jessie came that afternoon she asked me to go with her to extend condolences to the parents of two drowned boys who lived on top of Happy Top. I learned the whole story as we climbed the wagon trail up the mountain. They had picked blackberries that morning and taken them into town to sell and buy a sack of flour and sugar for the family. Then before going back up the mountain, they decided to do what their father had always told them to do to learn to swim. They told the clerk who had sold them the groceries all about it, that they would just jump in the water over their heads and start swimming. When their overalls were found on the bank with the flour, sugar and a bag of penny candy, boys who spent their summers in the river dragged it, and found the bodies for the county to bury. There was to be a three day delay in burying the bodies to enable relatives from "Dee-troit" to attend the funerals.

I was hot and thirsty when we finally got to the tar paper shack atop the mountain, but water was not to be had unless I'd do like everybody else--drink from a brown stained gourd kept at the family spring over which mosquitoes hummed and "skeeters" skipped. I rested for awhile under the shade of a hickory nut tree before following Miz Jessie into the house. Everyone seemed to be collected in cane bottom chairs on the front porch, but I saw the mother take Miz Jessie aside and tell her something needed to be done to the bodies to make them keep until the burials. Miz Jessie assured her she knew what to do to unembalmed bodies and I'd help her.

When we entered the room, the odor of a cloyingly sweet perfume combined with the odor of decomposition hit me and I began to wretch. Stoically Miz Jessie began to tap the sides of the open cardboard caskets to get the joints back together. They had had a hard trip in a wagon up the mountain trail. As she tapped, flies began to swarm above us from the blue netting covering the caskets. A thick brown liquid was seen oozing from the mouths of the swollen bodies. Miz Jessie said she should drain some of the contents of the stomach and would I find her a pan. I hurried to the back porch and got a fresh breath of air before looking for a pan. A dish pan was hanging on the wall but I took my time in getting it down to return to the room of awfulness.

Miz Jessie laughed as I gagged while holding the pan to catch the contents she was pushing into the pan. Finally I could stand it no longer, turned loose of the pan, dropped my handkerchief with the thirty-five cents in it, and ran to the outside to finish vomiting. At length, I returned to retrieve my handkerchief, but it was no longer

there. But the following Sunday, the day I was to return home, Miz
Jessie displayed my handkerchief nicely laundered and starched on
the bosom of her dress.

Atee's church flourished under the pastorage of Brother Nathan
and Miz Jessie's mission. The new church was erected, complete
with Sunday School rooms, electricity, electric organ, and out house.
Brother Nathan quit selling seeds to spend full time with his new
occupation. He went to the mission every other Sunday night while
Atee conducted the evening service at the Riverside church.

It was about a year later that an unfortunate event occurred. Atee
got a substitute for her evening service and asked my father to take
her to the back side of the mountain so she could attend the mission
service. He thought it would be a good outing for all of us so we had
a picnic along the road in order to get there in time for the service.

When we arrived, much to Atee's alarm, there were no lights on
and no people. Stumbling through the hut she encountered Brother
Nathan enjoying the bliss of Miz Jessie's bed. The conversation
which ensued was never related to me, but I'm sure she was looking
through the long range half of her bifocals, wiping the froth from the
corners of her drooping mouth with her turkey waddle in spasm as
she watched them dress and drive off in Brother Nathan's car. They
were never heard of again, though Atee's postulations of the work of
the devil were to continue for several months.

Several preachers were to come and go from Atee's church before
she finally "took to one". He proved to have a magnetic psychopathic
temperament that would have put the best con artist to shame. But
to give the devil his dues, he was the only person who ever out-

maneuvered Atee. He said he had been a boxer, deputy sheriff, and barn-stormer before he got "the call" to preach. I wondered if Atee's butter and egg supply in those depression years had anything to do with his "call", but he really filled the church. His rapport with the membership was so good that he quietly got them to remove Atee's name from the church roll.

For a time I felt sorry for her, but at the same time, I knew the joy the church felt to be rid of her dictatorial manipulation. But without the financial support from their corner pillar, they were doomed to failure.

When the church swarmed like a hive of bees, the practical members remained and the others went back to the foot-washing church. Atee was re-instated with full privileges of secretary-treasurer, superintendent of the Sunday School, and several other minor offices. Her sardonic humility on her return was anticipated from her interim remarks, "God will punish them for their sins", and,"They will miss me after a while."

The years elapsed without change, and it became time for Atee and Mother to get me ready for college. A newly purchased trunk from Sears, Roebuck had to be filled with "nice home made things" because this was standard when they went to Normal School. One of the first dresses I had to try on was an orange silk piquet with big puff sleeves, big black buttons and belt. I couldn't keep from cringing and said, "It's so loud they will see me coming a mile away."

"But its your school colors. You just don't know how you'll be admired when you get there", Atee said. It stayed in the bottom of my trunk all year, but the feed sack underwear was used because I had no other.

While Atee was basking in martyred glee in preparing me for college, Uncle Em was undergoing a period of trauma. He took his politics as seriously as Atee took her church. He was a perennial election officer and an August primary election was due. On election day he set off before day break to arrive at 5 a.m. in order to open the polls. But, no one was there and no one came while he squatted on his heels for two hours. Finally four drunk men staggered by and began to laugh. Uncle Em rose and asked where they had gotten the liquor. They told him where the other election officers had moved the polls to about two miles away. Silently, he walked away at a rapid clip for his eighty years. When he arrived at the new polling place he found the other election officers stuffing the ballot boxes. His tongue, ordinarily used only for chewing and spitting, suddenly loosed itself with curses and invectives never heard from him before, as he pulled a switch blade from his pocket and started toward the cheaters. A number of by-standers joined in the struggle to disarm him, but it was not until they agreed to let Uncle Em vote as many ballots as they had that Uncle Em calmed down. His side won his precinct by less than a dozen votes.

Atee was a prolific letter writer when I first went to college. Her excuse was that she thought I'd be home sick, but I never had the courage to tell her how glad I was to be away from home and her questions.

When spring arrived during my first year of college, I was horrified to receive a letter announcing her plan to come visit me because she wanted to meet my teachers and bring me a present. I suffered a month of dread before her arrival, and in spite of my detailed planning, I was unable to intercept her at the bus station and hustle her off to my room. She had purposely taken an earlier bus because she wanted to see me on campus as I usually behaved. I was on duty in the upstairs reference library when I heard a penetrating soprano voice saying, "And when she was three years old she would say, I fell down my grandma's steps and broke free of my teeth out, and when she was five she used to say, if they won't let me in the first grade, I'll just go on to high school, and if they won't let me go there, I'll just go on to college." I died a thousand deaths as I ran to intercept her and hush her with a kiss on her bearded cheek. I blushed in observing the tolerant smiles of all the occupants of the library.

Atee's usual accoutrements of purse, sewing bag, umbrella, and peck basket added further to my juvenile humiliation, so with the approval of the librarian to prevent further disruption, we hurried out of the library, and I took her to see my room. The first thing she took out of her basket was a heavy wool jerkin knitted in a beautiful rope pattern, but this was ten years after girls quit wearing jerkins, and I had to swelter in it all day.

During our tour of the campus we only met two of my professors and they, fortunately, were in a hurry to get somewhere, so they were not subjected to any of the cute sayings of my childhood.

She then insisted on taking me to the corner hangout restaurant to buy me a treat. En route I told her we wouldn't go in the back because they play bridge there, but my attempt to be a cosmopolitan member of the group was devastated anyway. We perched on stools at the counter and I introduced Atee to the proprietress. Her response to the introduction was to ask if I was a good girl. The lady hesitantly answered in the affirmative. "What kind of ice cream do you have? She learned at an early age that coca colas were not good for your stomach, so she never drinks them."

"Is that right," the proprietress replied, "I think that is remarkable." My blush paled as I realized she was playing along with the game.

The only class that day which served as a welcome was physical education. I had so much pent up hostility I became the overwhelming winner in a badminton tournament.

On our walk back to the bus station I wanted to tell her I genuinely appreciated her love and concern for me, but her outspoken demand for praise and her attitude of always being right, made her uncomfortable to be around, but I couldn't tell her. This was my first awareness of the frailty of human relationships.

My firm resolve to be nicer to Atee was quickly aborted the following year when she and two of her Homemaker Club friends came to visit my sister and me in our two room apartment at the state university. Now the unsightly demeanor of beard, turkey waddle, obesity, and assortment of containers, was worsened by her now standing bent forward in an ape like stance. My sister and I had worried how we could manage all these people in our two little rooms for three days, but on Atee's initial survey of our facilities she began a lecture on frugality because we now used tooth paste instead of the salt and soda we had used in brushing our teeth at home. We managed to prepare a tasty supper for them, put the two friends in the double bed and Atee on the sofa in that room, so my sister and I slept on the floor in the kitchen. The bathroom was the closet space between the two rooms. We even got up early enough to make biscuits for them for breakfast before I left with the three of them to find their meeting place. I then went on to the library to do the studying I hadn't done the night before.

I hurried home right after my last class so I could help my sister get ready for the evening. To my surprise, Atee and both friends were there already and the friends announced they were going to leave as soon as a husband came with his car. They had heard enough from the state Home Demonstration Agent. We apologized for not being able to provide more comfortable lodging, and they soon departed. Knowing Atee would insist on leftovers from the evening before, I fried potato cakes from the mashed potatoes, chopped up okra into the tomatoes, made corn bread, and made gravy for the cold roast beef. She was happy. My sister slept on the sofa and I held on to the rising half of the double bed because Atee's half was almost on the floor.

The next morning Atee told me she didn't want to take a tour of the campus because it was too big, but would I please take her to the art museum. I insisted the paleontology museum was closer and maybe she would like to see something she had never seen. I knew that museum rarely had many people going through it but she insisted on it being art. She commented on how worldly I was to be able to operate the elevator. When we started through the displays she would step back about three feet, close one eye, and circle the other eye with her cupped hand. I asked why she did that and learned her art teacher at Normal School had taught her that was the way real artists looked at paintings. I had no further comments.

The pseudo-sophistication of my senior year brought my first open rebellion against Atee. My visits home had become less frequent because Atee always arrived when I did and hours of questions were becoming intolerable. Occasionally I could stop the questions by reciting in alphabetic order all of the chemical elements and their symbols or saying the Prologue to the Canterbury Tales in old English.

At spring vacation my first evening home was awful. "Why haven't you had your church membership moved to where you live?" "What will it profit a man to gain the whole world and lose his own soul?" Don't you know the penalty of the eternal fire if you fall from grace?" "Think of the joy of sitting on the right hand of God singing hymns of praise to Him who created heaven and earth."

Hastily I replied, "I can't think of anything more boring. Imagine an eternity with the sanctimonious churchgoers who tag as a sin everything interesting and enjoyable."

"You can't mean that. But God will forgive you for thinking that and I forgive you for saying it," Atee said.

My father suddenly roused from his dozing attitude from behind a newspaper, saying, "Guess I'd better take you home, Atee, for I was already asleep. I'll go warm up the car."

Gathering up her paraphernalia, she withdrew a ten dollar bill and handed it to me. Nothing would have been more useful than ten dollars, but returning it to her basket I remarked, "I don't want your obligatory gift. I don't ever want to be obliged to you."

Tears welled up in her eyes, and peering at me through the long range half of her bifocals she meekly asked, "What have I ever done to offend you when you know I love you better than life itself?"

I was wilting in resolve but pursed my lips and said, "If you don't know there is no point in telling you." My father was honking his horn while we both stood eyeing each other, she with a hurt shocked look, while I tried to maintain a firm exterior to belie my quivering interior, and without another word, she made her departure. Time, distance, and fate have a way of dimming crises so there was never another confrontation between us.

Four years later, shortly after I had started work at the local hospital, a granddaughter of Uncle Em called me at the hospital to ask if I would arrange for Uncle Em to get into the hospital because, "He can't pee no more." A Urologist was called from a medical center who came to the hospital and surgically corrected his enlarged prostate gland. Atee enjoyed a profound exhibition of reunion when she realized I bore her no apparent ill-will. She was, however, somewhat more guarded in her lectures and questions.

Several weeks later I was dozing in the back of the early morning bus en route to work when I was aroused by an entering passenger in a penetrating soprano voice commanding, "Young man, don't you know you'll go straight to hell for smoking that cigarette?" I scooted lower in my seat because I knew it was Atee. Fortunately she found a seat in the front of the bus and exited before I did.

Uncle Em performed one more act which caused Atee much consternation. He sold off five acres of good bottom land at a price far in excess of its value for a farm. A small part of it was used to build an armature winding factory, but the remainder became a drive-in theater. On many occasions Atee stated to anyone who would listen, "Imagine them putting in that den of iniquity! The smoking and cursing that goes on there is a sight to behold. And think of the fornicatin' that goes on there in those cars after dark. Why, it's a veritable Hell-Hole!"

If Atee married Uncle Em because he was old and had financial security, she paid dearly for her greed. He lived for forty years after their marriage, and the last two years were composed of such abusive, belligerent behavior that it became necessary to put him into a state mental institution until sufficient male nurses could be hired to afford him the dignity of dying at home. After he was deposited beneath an angel adorned head-stone in the family cemetery, Atee wasted no time in obtaining a new charge to manage. Her recently widowed elder sister, Aunt Wilma moved in with her.

I only saw Atee twice after Uncle Em died. The first was several months after I became married to a high school English teacher. At the insistence of Mother, and unable to find an excuse to avoid the visit, I arrived with him to find Aunt Wilma in a rocker and Atee on the swing of the front porch. "Well, here he is for you to see," I stated. Previously I had informed her by letter that he would be the family black sheep because he was a Republican and a Unitarian. Without further greeting of any kind, Atee began to swing higher and higher as she recited the many verses of Gunga Din. We had in the interim taken seats as we grinned uncomfortably to each other, then my husband sought the security of a cigarette.

The swing began to slow and Atee said, "Young man, I was hoping you wouldn't do that."

Aunt Wilma interceded, "Now leave him alone, Atee. He's old enough to know what he wants to do and besides I like to smell it."

Family peace was finally established when they learned we now went to the Presbyterian Church, but we couldn't leave until my husband had not only given them the Welch origin of his name, but also five generations of both sides of his family tree.

Some years later, friends from the west became intrigued with Appalachia and particularly Atee, so we decided to expose them to it all first hand. We elected to take them in the fall because of the beauty of the mountains at that time. When we entered the stale aroma of old people, my husband devilishly introduced them by the name of Winemiller, rather than the afore agreed upon name of Miller. Aunt Wilma rose with agility for her 93 years, and shook hands. Atee ignored them and told me to kiss her. Then she turned her attention to our guests and pronounced their name, Winemueller. For about three minutes she talked nothing but German. Mr. Winemiller interrupted her to explain his family had been in this country for three generations and he didn't know a word of German.

Atee removed a switch blade from an orange crate next to her chair and began to pare her nails. Mr. Winemiller was noted to be having difficulty maintaining a courteous composure and reached into a magazine stand near his chair. Atee had returned her attention to me while Mr Winemiller hid behind the newspaper he had retrieved. He then spoke up, "Well, what do you know. Wilson is dead." When none of us could grasp his point he turned the paper for us to read the six inch headlines. With a smile on his face he said, "I'm so glad you saved this 1929 paper for me to read in 1966.

Atee then offered refreshments. "I've got a whole quart of good sweet milk not even pasteurized, and it wouldn't take long to fix tomato sandwiches to put on those paper plates I washed after your brother was here a month ago," she said. We refused because the many miles we still had to travel on our tour and made our departure.

I continued to get an occasional letter from her and learned only that her most prized possession was the fifty year pin her school had awarded her even though it was now a state university. I once suggested she write her memoirs to find some happiness in the years before I knew her, but to my knowledge that was never done. Both she and Aunt Wilma lived into their nineties but I didn't attend the funeral of either of them.

Chapter XII

Love Lifted Me

The sound of a cast iron stove lid hurled against the wall and gradually settling to the floor always indicated the onset of another melee at the Lily house which was across the road and about thirty yards up the hill in front of our house. Even above the clamor of the stove lid gyrating to gravitational force, Miz Lily's expletive loaded accusations of her husband, Joe, could be heard. The clang of more metal objects was always followed by the sound of breaking glass before Miz Lily would firmly announce, "Pappy, if ye touch airy one of them younguns I'll kill you with this butcher knife." Low pitched curses were then audible before the slam of a door and Mr. Lily could then be seen to stagger down the path to his blacksmith shop to sleep it off amid the bent nails and rusty iron scraps strewn on his work ledge.

It may seem strange that I would annex Miz Lily as a substitute mother, but her innately happy nature, and her "spade is a spade" approach to life and sex were prominent factors. Once she caught her youngest daughter, Little Eileen, and me in their two hole outhouse smoking rabbit baccer we'd rolled into cigarettes in brown paper. She emitted a chuckle while we tried to discard them and gain some composure, and then she said, "Child, yer mammy will be awful mad if she smells smoke on ye when you go home, so when you've had enough, come in and I'll rub some pennyroyal on you to hide it. Tryin' smokin' and gittin' sick is all part of bein' a youngun, so ain't no sense in gittin' a whoopin' too." The treatment worked and my mother never knew. This was quite a feat because my mother implied that she had a direct line to God and always knew when I thought evil even before I committed it.

I was always forbidden to associate with Miz Lily or play with any of her ten children. When I would ask why, Mother's answer was always that the Lily's thought differently from us, and indeed they did, for Miz Lily was invaluable in my sex education.

Miz Lily was a pretty little woman, barely five feet tall, whose age could have been anywhere from thirty to fifty. Her wavy black hair, loosely tied in a bun on the nape of her neck, had clean silvery streaks, and while her face had no wrinkles, it still bore a weathered look. Her markedly bowed legs were visible in her rapid six-inch steps, despite her ankle length faded gingham dress and snow white apron. She spat snuff juice so neatly from between her two front teeth that I always wanted to mimic her, but I never dared.

My sneaked visits were originated in my upstairs bedroom where I would go to read. I would push out the screen on the window, and crawl on the roof to the back of the house to reach the roof of the outhouse where I could ease myself to the ground, traverse the chicken yard and climb up the hill where a large pawpaw patch blocked the view from our front porch.

Little Eileen was a year older than me and skinny as a stray dog. Her thin light brown hair was parted in the middle and fell straight down to below her ears. Her teeth were slightly separated in the front and her big brown eyes would follow every move I made. Her hand movements were so swift she was the champion at ball and jacks before she ever started to school. I envied her most on May Day because she won every race she entered. She knew things I'd never find in books, some of them naughty, and one word she taught me that remained in my vocabulary for life was, "plike", which meant play-like, for indeed, she had a vivid imagination. Aside from the lure of having to sneak away from home to play with her, the other attraction was the place she had to play under their house. Here in the isolation created by the hillside in the rear, the porch floor above, and the rambling rose which hid the gaps in the under-pinning in front, we could dig tunnels, mold castles, make play dishes and furniture from the special type of clay it contained.

I was seven years old on the rainy day in which my education to real adult life began. We had just completed a funeral and burial of my Chinese rag doll, Su Foo Ming, or something that was supposed to mean, "God loves little children". This doll had been the gift from one of the endless number of missionaries who stayed with us when they toured the mountain churches to improve collections for their cause. I didn't like the missionary and her gift was equally distasteful. When this ritual was over we scratched in the clay while we wondered what to do next. Then Little Eileen said, "Did you know Pappy never finished payin' fer me and the doctor might come and take me back?" After my expressed disbelief, she added, "Mammy says I oughtn't worry about it, 'cause if the doctor wanted me back he'd have to put me inside a woman so's I could be birthed again, and she didn't reckon he'd want to do that." I still accused her of too much imagination so she insisted I go ask her mother. "You can ask her that and how she hid my oldest brother under a rock when her and Pappy got married."

We scooted through the absent under-pinning and climbed into the house of beds In the front room, a coal grate with two rocking chairs along side it filled a third of the room, and a small chest of drawers and a double bed completed the furnishings. The dining room had a pie safe, a long double board table on saw horses, two hickory cane bottomed chairs, and two long backless benches. The kitchen contained a large coal stove, a cabinet with a flour bin in the top segment and a very chipped enamel work ledge, a stand for the water bucket and tin wash basin, and a wobbly wooden table. Three flat irons which were heated on the stove during use were always a part of the kitchen decor.

When we entered the front porch Miz Lily was planting moss roses in an enamel wash basin which always shared the porch decoration with a worn out slop jar full of white petunias. She asked what we were up to and I couldn't say a word. Little Eileen giggled while

I told her how pretty the moss roses were. Finally I blurted out, "Little Eileen said you hid Fred under a rock while you and Pappy got married." When I saw her begin to chuckle from deep inside, I added, "She said the doctor might come and take her back 'cause you still owe him for her."

Miz Lily's chuckle became a knee slapping laugh while I uncomfortably brushed grit off the banister rail. She filled her lip with snuff, picked up a funeral fan and settled into a rocking chair before she asked, "Child, do ye know about where babies come from?" After she learned I knew that women split open for a baby to get out, she fanned herself for awhile, spat snuff juice over the banister rail and began--"I growed up down in Tennessee and wuz the first girl, number six, in a family of fifteen. When I was fourteen, this boy who was a heap older than me started hangin' around and axed me to marry him. Then his mammy come by one day to eat watermelon with us and when nobody else wuz payin' any attention, she told me she'd like fer me to come live at her house. That sounded good to me 'cause they wuz jest six of them so I knowed I wouldn't have half the washin' and ironin' I had to do at home. When I axed her if she wanted me fer a hired girl, she said she wanted me fer a daughter-in-law, so I said I'd ask Mammy." Miz Lily spat over the banister again and chased their mutt dog off the porch before she continued. "Well, Mammy said I might as well marry him, so we used up all the feed sacks we had makin' things fer me before we went to the Justice of the Peace that fall to get married. When we got to his house afterward, his mammy give us a room with jest one bed in it. I didn't think nothin' 'bout it 'cause I'd slept in a bed with brothers all my life, but then he commenced pawin' around on me and kept tryin' to kiss me. He even tried to take my clothes off and it wuz already cold weather. Finally he let me take off my coat and shoes and git in the bed and I wuz about half asleep 'fore he started foolin' around with me again. Well, I got plain mad then and jumped out of that bed, slapped his face, put my shoes on and walked the four miles home in the pitch dark."

I was so wrapped up in her story I didn't hear the quarrel two of her older children were having inside until she left to twist the ears of the boys to settle the dispute. Then after another spit of amber juice she continued, "Well, next mornin' when Mammy seed me makin' biscuits she axed why I'd come home. I told her what that man did and she didn't do nothin' but laugh at me and say that's the way men is. Later on that mornin' while I wuz scrubbin' on the wash board, she tried to tell me that lettin' yer husband git inside your clothes was how you paid him fer puttin' vitals on the table and a roof over your head. That evenin' he come to see me and I told him I didn't want to be married to him no more, and a few weeks later the "law" come and give me a piece of paper that said I warn't married no more."

She stopped her narration long enough for Little Eileen to bring her a gourd dipper full of water, part of which she drank and the remainder was poured on the newly planted moss roses. Then she continued. "I wuz fifteen years old when another boy started follerin' me to church and hangin' around the house, and I'd started gittin' my monthlys by then; so when he axed me to marry him I told him I'd try, but if I didn't like what he done, I'd quit bein' married to him. When I look back on it now, I guess I ought to a stayed married to him, 'cause he wuz a good boy and worked hard in the loggin' woods. After about six weeks I told him I'd rather wash and iron all day at home than to do that every night, so I went home to Mammy again and he never come to git me."

She put a pinch of snuff inside her lip and sat smiling for awhile. "I wuz eighteen year old when Mammy hired me out to work in a Boarding House at the saw mill. The World War was goin' on and most of my brothers had joined up so we didn't have much laundry and cookin' to do no more. Well, Joe lived at the Boarding House and worked on the new-fangled gasoline machines at the sawmill. He didn't talk much, but when he got cleaned up, he wuz the best lookin' man I'd ever seed. They wuz gittin' ready to move the sawmill to another place when he axed me to marry him, and I told him plain out, I'd been married twice and didn't like it either time, so maybe I ought to try him out fore I decided. He took me up to the pawpaw patch behind the Boarding House. God-a-mighty, child, he knowed just what to do, 'cause I never before had felt anything as good as that. 'Course I never dreamed I'd git a baby from the first time with him, but by the time he got back from the new sawmill to marry me, I looked like I wuz sproutin' a watermelon." All three of us enjoyed a good laugh.

"As to why I told Little Eileen Fred was hidden under a rock while we got married was because I'd either have to put a lie in the Bible or expect her to never learn to add and subtract, 'cause we got married just two months before Fred was born. I made sure all my younguns knew more than I did about where babies come from and how they get here than I did when I was growing up." She went on to say that having a baby didn't cause much more cramping than a big dose of castor oil and it was an awfully good feeling to see that baby come out crying. And in response to my question of how a baby got started, she used the words peter and snatch for penis and vagina, and without question this union wasn't always a nasty sinful act.

My mother was calling for me from our front porch so I ran down through the pawpaw patch, across the road and back to the outhouse so as to be able to pretend I'd been reading the Sears Roebuck catalogue we used for toilet paper in the out-house. When Mother told me to clean up the cow's stall and drive her down from the field so she could be milked, I didn't complain because I had lots to think about.

It was a few weeks after this that my sister and I were awakened by sporadic screams, groans and pleas for God's help coming from a house across the creek at the foot of the other mountain which enclosed us. We soon concluded this was John Bugler's house and because the screams and pleas were becoming louder and more frequent, we awakened Mother. We were sure she would want to do the neighborly thing and go help. Instead, she sat by the window and muttered only that she couldn't imagine what it was all about. When we ask if she should go see she told us she'd ask Dad and disappeared for the remainder of the night.

John Bugler was an elderly widower of near seventy when he brought home a roly-poly wife from the county seat. John had continued to tend his hillside farm and go to the A &P to buy double loaves of bread as was his custom. About the only time we saw his new wife was when she swept the front porch of their pealing yellow two story house while we played in the creek in front of it.

Finally we saw a car arrive and heard the doctor's voice between increasing grunts and groans of a woman. My sister and I concluded it had taken a while for the doctor's shot to work because it was a full hour before all was quiet and the doctor left.

Sleep did not come promptly when I returned to bed because of the memory of those signs of distress and Mother's atypical behavior during a crisis in our hollow. Next morning my unanswered questions were resolved and my regard for Mother's honesty fell to zero.

Mother and I were en route to do the morning milking, and as usual, Miz Lily and Little Eileen were on the hill above for the same purpose. Instead of Miz Lily's standard announcement of the beauty of the morning she yelled, "Reckon you know Miz Bugler had a pretty little red headed baby girl last night." Mother said she didn't know it but wasn't that nice. "You'd a thought she wuz the only woman in the world who'd ever birthed a youngun the way she carried on. I'm surprised you didn't hear her," she added. I could only look in stunned amazement when Mother told her she hadn't heard a thing. I never asked her why she lied, but henceforth if I wanted an honest answer to a question, I found some way to ask Miz Lily.

Miz Lily's happy disposition and her absence of complaint about their meager existence or Joe's spree drinking made her nice to be around. After everyone else in the hollow had electricity, she still had kerosene lamps, and while all other households had an electric iron, she was required to do her mammoth laundry with three little flat irons, for all in the family except Joe were always attired in starched unwrinkled clothes. Even though she was mostly happy she would mete punishment to her children, regardless of age or size. On one occasion she was in the middle of telling me a funny but naughty story about a once local lady of letters, who on returning for a family re-union fell in love with a "moon-eyed" half wit of half her age. Then her six foot tall high school senior son came storming onto the porch and yelled that his mammy had raised a bunch of uncivilized good-for-nothing animals. Miz Lily jumped up and grabbed him by his slicked down hair, pulled him down and cuffed his head and ears with her knuckles. After he begged her to stop she said, "Now you little turd, set down here and tell me what's eatin' on ye." He related that a half dollar he had in his box under his bed had been stolen and he had saved it to spend on the date he had for that afternoon. She sent Little Eileen to get her pocket book and emptied all the coins into his hands. Possibly she had folding money inside her bosom, but from all appearance, she was now penniless. Promptly she filled her lip with snuff, chuckled and resumed her story. As was usually the case, the once local lady of letters made a fool of herself over the laughed at local dullard because of his sexual equipment and prowess. This was incomprehensible to me at the age of eight, and so I continued to listen agog, acquiring a mounting catalogue of facts and intrigue to roam unsorted in the convolutions of my cerebrum.

Another trait of Miz Lily's which I appreciated was her ability to fit words into her speech which were totally taboo at home. I never registered these as curse words and her favorite expression "God a-mighty, Child" served only as underlining for her next sentence.

Once I was spanked for using this expression at home and I was told to never associate with any of the Lilys again.

As my fondness and dependency on the happy, forthright, energetic and compassionate Miz Lily grew, so did my comprehension of the curse she bore because of the behavior of her husband, Joe. Little Eileen maintained her pappy could make anything run, and when I allowed he surely made me want to run, she specified she meant motors and machines. But he did scare me, for when he had on his horn-rimmed glasses with the cracks in the lenses, his eyes looked like mosaics. His silence was only broken by curses and I always expected him to heave a discarded piece of red hot iron at me instead of the shop floor. Between drinking sprees he somewhat provided for his family by "tinkering" on cars and machines. If dire straits existed on their credit, he would re-open his small coal mine from which he shot enough coal to push a few loads to the surface in his hand-fashioned mine car, then haul it in an askew truck of his own design and sell enough to neighbors to tide the family over the crisis. He spent the bulk of his time banging and cursing beneath the hood of a car or lying in oily grass on his back beneath the long spent wheeled conveyance. He seemed to spend days disemboweling the burned or disheveled wrecks he towed to the perimeter of his shop, but in the end he pushed the rejected components over the hill to biodegrade in view of our front porch. Promptly Mother would plant another rambling rose bush and we then had a vista of roses on the whole hillside. But when fenders and gas tanks accumulated on top of the roses, she threatened to plant a Cudzoo vine for surely "cudzoo and the devil would inherit the earth."

Mr Lily didn't stamp a trade mark on any of the cars and trucks he fashioned because everyone knew they were his construction. The deaf could hear them, the blind with only light and dark perception could see the blacker than night cloud of smoke belching from their rears, and while the steam which rushed from the capless radiator was reminiscent of a locomotive, their odiferous output was a cross between the acrid odor of burnt grease and rotten eggs, so all beholders of these contraptions knew they were not alive. These marvels in metal were gotten into motion by cranking, but it was not until expletives were added to the sinew and sweat that motion began, and when in motion they moved with the grace and pace of a string-halted horse. Possibly comparison with a fiddler crab would be appropriate because neither half of the folding hood was the same model or color of its counterpart, and its asymmetrical frame or truck bed made it look as though it was dancing sideways on its treadless tires.

Joe's best customer for these mobile marvels was Souie Sam, the most enterprising butcher in town. He lived and had his store in a structure which had once been a grist mill on the bank of a creek at the edge of town. The building had always required the periodic addition of braces to prevent its being swept away by the spring floods, but its location for him was ideal since he hung the slaughtered animals and chickens on the edge of the porch and washed them in the creek. Those of us who lived up the hollow knew that at least a hundred privies dangled their rear ends over the creek like the bottomless rear flap of rompers. The other big asset Souie Sam had was his becoming akin, by common law, to a clan of chicken and cattle thieves. Each evening just before dark, the clan would crank up one of Joe's mobile marvels and travel to the next county where they could quietly load cattle and chickens into the truck before the owners were aware of their losses. Next morning, the carcasses would be suspended from their creek bank gallows ready for quartering and cutting to order. These were real bargains for those whose aesthetic values were less than average, and since most all meats were fried to a dark brown they didn't worry about the creek debris.

I was probably nine years old when an awkward situation was created by Little Eileen that threatened to disrupt my access to her clay and mother. She wanted to be invited to eat supper with us and had already gotten permission for me to eat with them. For weeks I pondered how I could get Mother's permission when I wasn't supposed to have any contact with her. Finally I approached Mother with her compassion for the starving children of China and stated Little Eileen had told me at school she hadn't had a glass of milk for months. I reminded Mother that Little Eileen's spindly legs and arms proved she was as near starvation as the children of China. Mother's first idea was that we should give her a plate of food and milk on the front porch like she fed all the hobos who came to the door, but finally she relented and allowed her to join us at the table. It turned out to be such a nutritious meal that nobody ate much and the only conversation was Mother's recurrent urge to Little Eileen to eat more. It was not until I sneaked up the hill for my supper with them that I learned their meals would be wordless too.

Promptly at 4:30 PM, Mr. Lily came in from his shop and wordlessly proceeded to the waiting pan of water and lye soap to wash his grimy face and hands. Miz Lily and the girls promptly scurried to put jelly glasses of water beside each tin plate on the sawhorse table, and by the time Mr. Lily was seated in a cane bottomed chair at the end of the table, a large cake pan of square cut corn bread, a mammoth mixing bowl of soup beans, and a dish of onion slices were arranged before him. He began to load his plate while Miz Lily hurried to her place at the other end of the table and all the boys slid onto one bench and the girls on the other. When Mr. Lily had filled his plate with each item, he gave its container a shove on the table and the occupants of both benches grabbed to catch it. Each plate was filled without a word and each eater leaned elbow to elbow shoveling the bean soup soaked corn bread and slices of onion into his mouth a distance of six inches from the table top. The meal was over when the bean bowl had been spooned dry and the last crumb of corn bread had sopped up the last puddle of soup, then a hearty belch announced the exit of each.

As I neared adolescence, my relationship with Miz Lily became more symbiotic. I realized she had the capacity to worry but the fortitude not to dwell on it. Her family had many times exhibited the trait that when their horn of plenty overflowed, they really "lived it up" and lolled in luxury. One day I was gathering ripe pawpaws when Little Eileen appeared licking an all-day sucker and boasting of another in her pocket. She gave the second one to me and announced she had lots more because one of her brothers had found a money tree on the back side of the mountain. My adamant insistence that money trees were no more real than Santa Claus prompted Little Eileen to elaborate so graphically on the contents of the tree and the attachment of the assorted prizes to the branches that I wanted to believe. For a short time period we reverted to early childhood as we sat on moss covered boulders licking the suckers and fashioning a world of splendor from the products of money trees, and it was with great sadness that my incessantly spinning wheels of logic brought an end to our dreams of luxuries. Little Eileen finally brought an end to our conflict with an invitation to hear it first hand from her Mammy, so adeptly we coursed our way over fallen logs and relished the soft velvet pile of moss on our bare feet to reach the tar paper home and Miz Lily on the front porch. My direct question to her about the money tree brought a little chuckle from her throat and she promptly directed Little Eileen to go to the spout for a bucket of water. Then she took me by the hand for a tour of the house. From beneath each bed she withdrew two new pairs of shoes and from beneath the girls' bed she brought out a bolt of dainty batiste to be made into dresses, a large box of chocolates, a pair of real silk hoses for herself, and a rainbow of lollipops and bubble gum.

When we returned to the porch I noticed some tears forming in her eyes while she filled her lip with snuff, and then she said," Child, that third oldest boy of mine is a good boy and I reckon he sure loves his old mammy and all the younguns. No, they aint no money tree and you knowed it a'ready, but he wouldn't tell me where he got all them thangs and a mammy ain't agoin' to accuse her own youngun of doin' some 'um bad. Maybe he got the money from a poker game, but I ain't about to tell the younguns he gambles." She spat over the banister and fanned herself a few times, and then added, "Looks like the children don't get a heap of the thangs they need, let alone thangs they don't need, so I figgered they might as well git the pleasure out of it while we wait to see what happens." To my knowledge, the Lily boy was never apprehended and not long afterward he enlisted in the army.

When I was ten years old and in the seventh grade, mother selected a new friend for me. Her name was Dorcus and each of her five siblings bore Biblical names which, according to Mother, showed their parent's dedication to a fine Christian upbringing for the children. Our mothers decided we should rotate homes for Sunday dinner and afternoon play. This arrangement brought us together for thirty hours of school each week, plus Wednesday night Prayer Meeting, Rainbow Girls after school on Thursday, and literally all day Sunday, which included four church sessions. When I asked to abdicate my place at Dorcas' Sunday dinner, her virtues of perfection and humility were so exclaimed that I was charged with my Christian duty to mimic her demeanor. If I had informed mother Dorcus giggled and said nasty things when she saw her little brother masturbate, she would have spanked me for fabricating. Nor did she know that Dorcus constantly copied my home work to turn it in at school. So thrown with her constantly, I soon began to enjoy the juicy tid-bits of gossip she seemed to know about everyone of our mutual acquaintance.

There was an older, well blossomed, frizzle-haired girl in the back of our class who was repeating the school year because she was so jumpy and nervous she couldn't learn. Her dress was always too exotic and her heels too high for our age group, so when Dorcus told me the girl was pregnant and didn't have a husband, I was amazed.

She pointed out the D cup bra she wore and the slightly rounded abdomen, so I couldn't wait to tell my older sister of my advanced knowledge. Unexpectedly, my sister became very angry, shamed me for spreading such terrible gossip, and refused to believe Dorcus had told me. Next morning at the beginning of school our teacher firmly bid me to come to the cloak room where she waited with my sister and the crying frizzle-haired girl. Confronted with being the source of the rumor, I insisted it was Dorcus who had told me, so she was added to the conference. Before my very eyes, Dorcus swore to God she knew nothing of the rumor until that very instant and expressed all manner of compassion for the frizzle-haired girl so unjustly treated. Humiliated and maligned, I apologized and complied with the teacher's order for me to hug the victim. I was sure I would catch the head lice which Dorcus had also said she had. My anger at the sanctimonious behavior of my sister made me hope I'd catch lice so I could give them to her. Silently I seethed for days, refusing, even with the threat of punishment, to attend any of the church meetings and I spoke to no one at school.

Finally the occasion arose when I could relate this episode to Miz Lily. Her leathery face remained unsmiling through my recitation and her questions. She fanned her face for a minute before she smiled and said, "I don't reckon ye told yer mammy none of this, and I don't reckon nobody ever told you it was a sister of that frizzle-haired girl who got pregnant by her daddy and he tried to blame it on a teacher so he could make some money." Then she chuckled from deep down inside and added, "If you'uz to tell anybody I said that I'd swear to God you'uz lying, so I'd make right shore you'd learnt yore lesson."

By this time I could laugh too and could listen unabashed to her advice. "Child, yer mammy and sister are a heap alike. Both of um high strung. I know yer mammy don't think much of me cause I ain't had the education she had, and they's times even my children think I'm the dumbest mortal on earth. But it don't do no good to keep on thinkin' on it. 'Sides ye ain't goin'a be livin' in the same house with yer mammy and sister much longer."

Ah, that last idea did it--it was hope, the eternal hope to be grown and independent, the yearn to join the adult fraternity where interests could be pursued without inhibition and thoughts could be expressed without fear of adult disapproval, so back to my normal passive, adult-doting self I returned to try to patiently await the age for my declaration of independence.

It was when the sap began to rise that spring that I dealt with a far more threatening peer provoked conflict than the episode with Dorcus and the frizzle-haired classmate. A biologically mature repeater from the back of the seventh grade room asked me to walk behind her to the girl's room so the boys wouldn't see the stain on the back of her dress. Blushing, I complied. I hadn't been to the girl's toilet room since I was in the second grade and acquired better bladder control, but the room looked the same as it had then. None of the toilets flushed. A door was missing from one of the four toilet booths, and the floor looked like the girls treated their excreta as if they were cows in a pasture. In short, it was a place where one would never try to walk barefooted.

I offered to wait out in the hall while she hop-scotched over the puddles and piles, but she insisted I wait in the room with her. Just as I found a place where I could lean against the wall, she made a large leap and grasped with one hand the bar over the door-less stall. Then suspending her clutch purse in her teeth to free the other hand, she did an about face on the bar and swung herself back to stand atop the dirty toilet seat, squatted, voided, removed her soiled sanitary napkin and flung it toward the far booth. When she announced she must wash her dress tail, she threw her purse to me, and again swung from the bar to an "unmanured" locus near a sink. Then leaping back to the stall bar she continued to swing endlessly, while giving me sex education I would never have found in books at home nor in the school library. It was knowledge which most ten year old girls would boast of in the days of the "knock, knock!" riddles.

Later I related the whole episode to Miz Lily so as to check on the veracity of the facts. Early in my recitation I began with her first "knock,knock!" to which I replied, "Who's there?" The inquisitor then stated, "Her Buster." My reply was to be, "Buster who?" She then said, "Buster cherry", and we both laughed but I didn't know why. Sensing my blushing ignorance, Miz Lily proceeded to tell me in unschooled terms all about the hymen, erections, ejaculations, the relationship of menstruation to pregnancy, and the incomparable bliss of sex, "as long as ye take keer of yerself so's ye don't get p.g." So the illiterate matron in our hollow who was to be avoided because "she thinks differently from us", repeatedly chuckled contagiously from deep inside through my long recitation to the point that Little Eileen joined us to see what was so funny. On completion Mz Lily dried her tears of laughter, filled her lip with snuff and began a most beautiful rumination on sex that I later re-phrased and used for sex education in the first Biology class I taught. It was then that sex neither became dutiful nor dirty, but a shared delight of love, and love itself acquired a definition that had nothing to do with looks, lust, wealth or social standing, but a kind of respect for each other. She admitted there were circumstances that sort of killed respect once held, but she went on to say, "A woman's got it all over men, "cause the younguns she gits from lovin' can't never be took away from her 'cept by death, and ye can live a awful long time without no man to love as long as ye got younguns to live for."

With my quandary of sex now replete with all the answers, I thought, the next couple of years could be spent in admiring Mz Lily's gradually improving economic state. The son who had joined the army first sent her a satin sofa pillow which had a gold lettered poem on it, and the first letter of each line spelled Mother. His next gift was a battery radio which went full volume from the five a.m. farm facts to the midnight Star Spangled Banner, until the battery ran out of juice and then we all enjoyed peace and quiet. Thereafter, the entire holler knew when her allotment check arrived because a new battery enabled all of us to turn off our radios and listen to the program of her choice.

Another of Miz Lily's sons graduated from high school as valedictorian and received full scholastic and athletic scholarships. She nearly burst with pride. My father gave him a summer job on the highway, so he went to college in new clothes and new suitcases. His mother did his laundry each week, ironing seven shirts with a flat iron heated on the stove, and mailed them back to him next day.

There were now three children away from home, ergo, one empty bed. The army son had another good poker session and sent money for a day bed with pillows to replace the bed in the living room. The old bedstead was used to encircle the graves of two children who had died of the summer Flux. Enclosing family graves was common practice to keep cows from grazing on the mounds.

The oldest Lily daughter got pregnant and married, and for some time it looked as though Miz Lily's perpetual happiness was gone. Maybe it was then I reciprocated some of the compassion she had expended on me, except I had no tools but listening to exhibit my concern. Tearfully she spat and said, "I know I ain't got no room to be mad at her for gettin' pregnant, 'cause I done it myself, and it shore looks like all my chickens is coming home to roost. But child, I'd a heap rather she stay home and let me help her hold her head up. I know there ain't a house in the world big enough to hold two grown women, but I jest got a uneasy feeling about that man she married."

The uneasy feeling about her new son-in-law proved justified. Shortly after the baby was born, her husband got drunk and took her for a car ride and crashed her side of the car into a tree. For several weeks she was in the hospital and her survival was in doubt. Finally she began to rally and was left with one leg that wouldn't bend. When I paid a visit after she had returned from her daughter's home, she said, "He's quit drinking and acts like he's going to buy her everything she wants, but, Child, I still ain't going to give him no more rope than it takes to hang him. My girl says he done it 'cause he was jealous, and he still acts crazy about her. He does his own cooking and won't let nobody touch anything he has bought to eat. I shore wish I hadn't told my girls they'd have to lay in the beds they had made for theirselves."

As the months wore on, and the crippled daughter became more obese, her husband's paranoid behavior waned and Miz Lily's chuckles from deep inside returned. She finally included grandchild and son-in-law in the mantle gallery she displayed at each of my visits.

There was one more episode in my growing up when Miz Lily was a real friend and stabilizer for me. My sister and I were now of equal progression in high school, and the community had many times informed me I would have a nervous breakdown because my parents were letting me go through school too rapidly. My sister was already well advanced in an adolescent rebellion against our parents, and the only way I could avoid the tension was to run to my room and hide in a book. I was also in the awkward position of being the mediator between my sister and mother. Objectively, each had a measure of merit on her side, but neither would budge an inch.

The breaking straw occurred when Mother required Dad to spank Karla and tell her she must never associate with her two close friends because they had been seen smoking and dancing in public. My sister cried for two days, and then as if nothing had happened, she became the model sister and daughter for three days.

On that fateful early evening I was roused from a book by a most dreadful scream of my sister rushing down stairs pleading for someone to stop the burning in her throat. Apparently my father recognized the odor of Lysol or saw the furrowed burn on her lip, for without a word, he picked up a dipper and made her drink cold dirty dishwater. After forcing a gallon down her, he rammed his fingers down her throat to make her vomit. He followed this with a pint of whipping cream, and then he and mother took her to the hospital.

I was glad to have all the evening chores to do because I could cry at will and no one would know. I considered all the what if's for my sister, and prayed that she get well. If she was seriously injured for life because our parents didn't want her to associate with two stupid girls who would probably not graduate from high school, it would be a travesty. For that matter, whether she lives or dies, what will I say at school tomorrow because everyone will know.

For years I wished my mother hadn't said what she did when they returned home at midnight. The doctor had assured them she would live, but she might have to have a hole cut into her stomach to be able to eat, and then "It's the best thing that could have happened because now she will listen to what her Daddy and I have to say", she said. I looked in dumb amazement and was too startled to reply. I thought of the suicide note I had found which said only that she couldn't live without friends.

"If I have to go to school tomorrow, I better go to bed, I announced with all the calm I could muster. I accepted her dutiful peck on the forehead and her reminder to say my prayers, and left the choking atmosphere of the woman who said she was our all loving mother. The confusion of my thinking and the groping for a pure emotion to grasp or an ideal to hold on to consumed the hours until daybreak when the happy sounding boast of a neighbor's Bantam rooster seemed to arouse some hope in me which was too vague to define. I lied at breakfast and said I'd had a good night of sleep, and then listened to Mother's drone about what a bad night she had endured.

Just as I was ready to leave for school, Mother said, "You must tell your sister's two friends they must not associate with her again."

"But, Mother, do you realize what you are asking?"

"Don't you love your sister?" she replied.

God, here I was trapped again as if she had used her age old retort, "So I've lied then, have I?"

I said I'd do it and I did, but not in the words demanded. It was no more painful then the walk to school with everyone asking what had happened to my sister. Her two friends seated themselves on either side on me at the first period. I just told them mother didn't approve of them smoking and had forbidden them to associate with my sister any more. They were shocked, but not shocked enough to restrain from copying my test paper in that class.

That evening my parents were at the hospital again, and I finished all the chores much too fast. Reading was impossible and roaming from room to room only evoked echoes of "It's the best thing that could have happened to her." I went out to the roadside ditch to flick gravel at the tadpoles and breathe air not tainted with parental sounds, and air which would not oppress or suffocate. Then Miz Lily called and I went straight up the hill to her house without looking back to see if I'd been caught. She showed me the new pictures on the mantle first and then the new armed chair which now shared the spotlight with the daybed in the front room. Then she said, "Them doctors will make your sister git well, and I know everybody is tellin' yer mammy and pappy how sorry they are, and I reckon they ain't nobody thinkin' about you." I thanked her and assured her I'd be all right, but I still couldn't tell her what mother had said that first night at home. She apparently guessed some of it, for her next sentence was, "Child, I told you a long time ago, your mammy and sister are a heap alike, and both of 'um is awful high strung. Of course I can't say I know more about raisin' younguns than she does, and she's had a whole lot more larnin' than me, but I figure whatever came up twixt yer mammy and sister was just because yer mammy was tryin' too hard to make you all grow up before your time. 'Course growin' up ain't easy for nobody, and I reckon it's as hard on mammies as it is on younguns." I smiled and nodded but still couldn't give a reply. Miz Lily added, "I been doin' a heap of thinkin' since that loud mouth woman in town told you you'd have a nervous breakdown for gittin' through school too soon, but God A Mighty, Child, they ain't no sense in that. I'd whip you myself if you tried to. The way I figure things is you done lived through the worst of your life, and from now on, you can figure out things for yourself."

Miz Lily hadn't resolved all my dilemma, but she had introduced that most valuable asset to living--hope. Asserting that I could now count on one hand the years which must elapse before my declaration of independence, I could then accept a piece of jam cake and Kool-Aid to assuage my unrecognized hunger.

When my sister came home from the hospital a few days later without need for surgery, a prescribed ulcer diet provided a means of pampering without parental concession to humility, and gradually the unspoken strain of adjustment became tolerable enough to be unnoticeable.

Resolving the smoldering disdain created by Mother's comment the night of the suicide episode had now become a consuming problem.

On the one side of the coin, I had been reminded too many times of the sacrifices she had made for us to consider being ungrateful. Still on the other side of the coin was the ingrained dogma that she had a direct line to God, and thus incapable of error, but most of all, my saturation with quotable scriptures made it the most carnal of sins to admit hating a human being, and especially to hate one's own mother. It was almost as if the divine right of motherhood were comparable to the divine rights of kings. The only argument on the obverse side of the coin was that Mother's actions and attitude had almost cost my sister's life. So for the final two years of my tenure under parental roof, my overt passiveness and reputation for being the perfect child was perpetuated while the conflict within me raged unabated. While a significant part of my thoughts and explorations had always been hidden from parental perusal, it now became a game to delude them.

Blessed are the therapeutic effects of the "wild oats" of college, and hallelujah for the day one can explode with an emotion repressed for eons; a phrase which shouts, "I hate". Thereafter the calm quiet bowel which follows that catharsis enables the peristaltic rhythm of emotion to function innately without schooled control. It is then the maturing child can say unabashed, "When I was a child I spoke as a child, I thought as a child, but when I became an adult, I put away childish things . . . , for finally hate can be replaced with compassion, hurt can be quelled with knowledge of constancy, awesomeness can be transformed into awareness of human frailty, and doggedness can be accepted as an endless strife against adversity. Then with the eventual admission that these new attributes connote love, the world becomes beautiful and life within it, while still gnarled with the intrigue of human fallibility, it all becomes worthwhile.

It was over two years before the swinging pendulum of emotion came to rest near mid-center and I was ready to try a visit home. We had barely finished a review of the births, deaths, marriages and divorces of old acquaintances when Miz Lily called from her tar paper house on the hill to tell me to come see her that minute. I gave mother a quizzical look, and to my surprise she agreed I should go. "When I last talked to her on our way to milk, I decided she wasn't half bad", she said.

I went straight up the hill to her house without looking back to see if I'd been caught. My sneak path to her house was over-grown but the memory of its contour enabled me to climb speedily there and receive the biggest hug I had ever had. She asked about my progress in school while she looked at me with teary-eyed pride. As I looked around the room, I commented how good everything looked and how much I wanted to see it all. We started with the new pictures on the mantle. Electricity glowed from every possible place and her front bed room now contained a closet and chest of drawers along with one bed. Only the back bed room still had two beds for grandchildren when they came to visit. The last room we saw was the kitchen, and there the three little flat irons still adorned the top of the coal stove. In response to my mentioning the flat irons, she said, "The younguns wanted me to throw them into the creek, but I told 'um, it just looks like I spent so many hours with them, it would be like throwin' a part of me in the creek."

Another of the vestiges of the past was the long saw-horse table, with benches, and pie safe. I drank coffee while I sat on the girl bench to watch the new china display in the pie safe. It began to dawn on me that she hadn't mentioned her husband, so I asked about him. My long face on learning he had died a year ago was soon erased when she said, "God-A-Mighty, Child, these has been the happiest days of my life since he died. "Course when I heard all that commotion in his shop and then everything was silent, I knowed he was dead. When I went to see about him, he'd knocked everything down when he fell. I fetched help but there wasn't nothing anybody could do. They's some folks think I'm mean for saying I'm happier now, but, Child, they ain't no use in making somebody bigger after he's dead than when he was alive." I could only nod agreement and sip coffee. Then she added, "Lot's of time I lay in bed at night and think about how much I thought of him when we first got married, and I reckon you know how mean he was to me and the younguns when he was drunk, and how much the younguns done without 'cause he wouldn't hardly do nothing but tinker with them old cars." Tears had reappeared in her eyes. She got up from the cane bottom chair at the foot of the saw-horse table and walked into the kitchen. I heard her remove the stove lid and spit into the fire. As she returned to the table she said, "I sure got myself a heap of mighty fine younguns out of it, and I'm awful proud of every one of them, and a little bit proud of you too."

I hugged and kissed her and asked her to remember me to her children before I made my departure. I returned to my biologic parents without ever telling her of her invaluable role in my upbringing.

Probably I thought I'd do it on my next visit home, but before that occurred, she had died in her sleep.

Chapter XIII

What Child Is This

No one bothered to inquire from which mining camp the Leas had come. A pick-up truck containing their household possessions and a residue of coal from its previous haul stopped in front of a long vacated, square, styleless house one day to install Mamma and Daddy Lea along with their three children into our hollow.

Quietly and rapidly they repaired broken window panes, painted the house a pale lipid yellow, exhibited a cooperative attitude at the community water spout when they went to bring in their "night water", and in no time it was as though they had, like the rocks and coal and pawpaw trees, always been there. But now the pawpaw trees and their late summer weapons of mushy black fruit are gone, the rocks and coal lie undisturbed, and three of the Leas lie in total conformity in the cemetery on Graveyard Hill, remembered only by a conforming son on Decoration Day.

The conforming son who, like his father, prefers silence rather than bear the brunt of community jokes because of his stammering speech, now occupies the neat styleless house with his wife and three children. Seeing the frugal, toneless existence of the son and his family gives one the impression of timelessness, as if the rampant changes of the past thirty years somehow passed over in the eye of a tornado and left this one acre plot with its inhabitants intact, untouched, and exactly as they existed in the 1930's.

Mamma Lea was a round woman in her thirty plus years who appeared much older because of the reddish-brown freckles on her always worried face. She was docile beyond comprehension, for her voice, even in anger, denoted pleasantness, and her admonitions were loaded with terms of endearment. Her redder than brown hair which was always pinned out of the way, was fine and sparse, but wisps of straight strands falling down on her moist neck provided channels for her constantly perspiring face. She was the sort of woman that everyone in the community knew, but no one thought to remember she existed unless she came into direct view. When this occurred she would swap woe for woe in discussion of ailments, lack of economic splendor, or the adversity of the weather with the most skilled members of the "I do declare" matrons in the neighborhood. There were no enemies to Mamma Lea, and yet, despite the fact that she promptly produced sounds of empathy and made generous contributions of gladiolas from her yard and ham from her smokehouse for every wake, there were no close friends. She had no one with whom she could sit on the porch on Saturday afternoon and click tongues of shamed amazement.

The house of the Leas was as non-controversial and unadmired as they. Each room, while hygienically clean, conformed in size, furniture, and homemaker adornments as were to be found in every other home of coal mining families in our isolated Appalachia.

While the four room house was under the jurisdiction of Mamma Lea, the only portion of the exterior which was not devoted to Daddy Lea's energetic effort to provide food for his family was the row of gladiolas and a row of coxcombs in the small grassless front yard. If their two boys were careful, they could spin tops or shoot marbles in this area. But mostly the boys were occupied with helping Daddy Lea tend the weedless garden, quick lime the pig pen to neutralize the odor of the wallowing larders, and help with the endless chore of bringing water from the spout.

Daddy Lea somehow exuded love and concern for the whole family, but all of them had an uncanny worship of Meritta, the daughter, and one always got the impression she was the center of their universe.

On July 4th, Daddy Lea always came home from town in a taxi laden with a case of cokes, a large watermelon to be cooled in a wash tub, and a gallon of ice cream already melting in the hot sun.

On Decoration Day the family dressed in their Sunday best clothes and went off in a taxi with crepe paper flowers they had made to place on the graves of their kin. Then on Labor Day they went off to celebrate the day in the festivities of the labor union to which Daddy Lea was required to belong. Prior to the attainment of a "closed shop" he seemed to approach labor affairs much as the family approached religion; they attended the Holiness Church but never put on an exhibition of having the Holy Ghost. When in the vicinity of churchy people they nodded approval but otherwise it was not apparent it interested them, and while they dutifully contributed their just tithe to God and John L Lewis, they appeared to expect no more from these contributions than from the money given to the insurance policy man each week. In fact, save for the enjoyed extravagance of Christmas, Easter, the Fourth of July, and Labor Day, the Lea parents were consumed with frugality and conformity. They bubbled with over-spilled pleasure in gifts to the three children at Christmas and Easter, especially so to Meritta who could be expected to parade at Easter the most expensive dress from the first glossy page of the Sears-Roebuck catalogue.

There were some areas of frugality which seemed to be carried beyond reason, but who is to judge. Maybe it was modesty instead of frugality that made Daddy Lea arrive home from the mine still wearing the carbide lamp on his cap, his dinner bucket suspended beneath his arm pit and his blackened skin indistinguishable from the underwear showing through his unbuttoned shirt. He would then fill a number two galvanized tub from the boiler steaming over an open fire in their back yard before shedding his black clothes and bathing in the galvanized tub in an unheated portion of the back porch he had partitioned off. For him to come home clean each day, the mining company would have withheld each month one and a half dollars ($1.50) for a locker and use of the community shower.

The Leas added a variation to the evening ritual in the hollow in late summer. Each family must take care of the evening chores of milking the cow, feeding the chickens, carrying in coal and kindling, and bringing enough water from the spout to last through the night and breakfast preparation. But all the children in the neighborhood liked to gather for one last game of marbles, hide-and-seek, or tops if they were in season, or sometimes to just sit on the hillside to dream of what life would be like when they grew up. When the sun fell over the apex of the mountain at the head of the hollow, each family had its own unique way of calling its children to get the chores completed and everyone gathered for supper. The pattern Mamma Lea used when she called Meritta was new to us. It would begin, "Meritta, honey, you come here, honey, or I'll cut the blood out of you, honey." Silence would then reign for several minutes and other mothers would begin to call their brood for the night. The assortment of calls was unexplained, but the twelve Smith children knew the first "Whoo Whoo" meant for them to come promptly, and a shrill whistle through the snuff stained teeth of Mz. Lily was only an alert. However, if the Lily children tarried after the second whistle, a louder coarser abrupt blast from Mr. Lily would soon be followed by the sound of a razor strap flaying against the seat of each Lily child.

Running a close second to the uniqueness of Mamma Lea's evening call was that of Mz Box calling Junior. It would begin with, "Woh, Junor, Jun-ner, you come here 'cause I got the cornbread on." With the next call one heard, "Junnry, Woh, Junnry! You git here 'cause supper's on the table." A few minutes later her more irate voice would call, "Now, Junnry,Damn your lazy hide. You answer me." Still silence would be followed by, "Now, Junnry, I know ye ain't much smart, but God blast your sorry hide, I ain't goin' stand here and call you all night." Occasionally Junior still failed to respond, and this would result in an explosion of expletives to enlarge the vocabulary of us all.

The calls of Mamma Lea continued until the day was suddenly night and the bare bulb over the kitchen table began to glow. We would then hear a scream of fear in the direction of Meritta's location, and Mamma Lea would begin to call, "Meritta, honey, just keep crying so's me and yer Daddy can find you. We're coming with a flashlight." When they arrived, Daddy Lea seemed to lose his stammer as he soothed Meritta's sobs while he carried her in his arms.

The only other trait which singled Meritta out from the rest of the children in our hollow was her daily temper tantrum. If there had been a Good Humor man driving through and she had been denied a treat, it might have been understandable, but there were no such menaces in those days in Appalachia. It seemed instead that these tantrums began at three pm and seemed to be provoked by Meritta's yen to put on her Sunday dress instead of the one selected by Mamma Lea, or by Meritta's impatience with her mother's clumsy hands when she would be brushing her Shirley Temple curls. All of us within hearing distance wanted Mamma Lea to prune a limb from their maple tree, and give Meritta something to cry about, but this crying usually continued a couple of hours when she went out to play. If she came to where we slightly older children were doing chores or playing, she would stand with a thumb in her mouth and not say a word. On occasion we would be so annoyed with her we would offer to let her play "Booger" with us.

Booger was a stupid little game in which we'd invite Meritta or any disliked small child to go up to the pawpaw patch with us to pick partially ripe fruit and offer it to the child. When the child's mouth began to pucker from the bitter tart taste we would apologize with tongue in cheek, and then we all squatted in a circle to tell "booger" stories. These were usually variations on the theme of Hansel and Gretel, but at the climax of the story when the "booger" appeared, we would suddenly scream and run off to hide in the twilight, leaving the panicked victim crying or running for home. Meritta never seemed to learn the game.

The only Monday Mamma Lea did not announce her dedication to the family's cleanliness with a long dangling array of union suits, shirts, dresses, and sheets on a clothes line suspended from the corner of the house to a tree was the day Mamma Lea entered the seven year old Meritta in school. Meritta was prancing in a new green taffeta dress, white gloves, and black patent leather shoes, while Mamma Lea bore an expression which seemed to say, look at my pretty little doll. It was an expression which would have erased the worry from her freckled face had her moist neck and wet armpits not betrayed her anxiety.

Other mothers and their first graders joined Mamma Lea and Meritta as they walked down the road, through town and then to the swing bridge which traversed the creek and three railroad tracks at the base of schoolhouse hill. Periodically Mamma Lea called endearing admonitions to Meritta as she was caught teasing her peers or prissing her wide-gored taffeta dress immodestly. When they arrived at the swinging bridge, Mamma Lea took Meritta's hand, but with the first step on the swaying structure, Meritta stopped and began crying while she clung to her mother's skirt. Some older boys in the middle of the bridge began to jump in order to make the bridge swing higher and higher, and began to chant, "First grade babies is skeered of the bridge." With a determined air, Mamma Lea picked up the crying child, and with a wide stance, walked silently past the chanting boys and set her down on the other side of the bridge. But Meritta's crying continued and she refused to move. It was not until Mamma Lea had picked her up again that she realized Meritta's panties were wet, but when she turned to start for home Meritta's crying ceased.

The next morning the dolled up Meritta was seen going to school holding a hand of each of her overalled brothers. It was not until near noon time that a brother was summoned to the first grade to take his wet sister home. In the course of the next few weeks, Meritta's bladder control improved and in the main she adapted to first grade life.

Lest the impression is created that Meritta was retarded in her toilet training, some of the physical features of the school require explanation: This was one of the first schools constructed in Appalachia which had inside plumbing and water fountains instead of an outhouse and hand pump with a community dipper. Consequently, there was a four stall toilet for the female students and teachers and another for the males for all twelve grades. The other problem accounting for the inadequacy of the sanitary facilities was that the elderly politically appointed janitor had never seen a toilet that flushed, so he could not be expected to know how to repair it. Additionally, by the time the summer time broken windows had been repaired in the fall, there was no money left in the school budget to repair broken plumbing. Had the toilet facilities not always been over-flowing, demanding more attention to where one stepped than that required in a cow pasture, the wisdom of placing the first grade classroom next to the toilet would have been lauded. Instead, the furnace room located on the other side of the first grade was lauded, for here the elderly janitor could look up from his Wild West magazine at intervals to inform the drying child it was time to rotate before the open door of the furnace.

Probably it was predictable that Meritta would be more concerned with peer admiration than with learning her ABC's. When called upon to do simple addition or pronounce the letters on a flash card, she stood sucking her thumb and silently dripping big tears, but during music period, she was the first to raise her hand to perform. Coming coyly forward with her blonde precise Shirley Temple curls and fussy, wide-gored skirt and matching bloomers, she tapped a brief, two-point dance, held out the hem of her skirt and began singing The Good Ship Lollipop. When adolescence approached she cultivated a cracked nasal twang and a mike-holding stance to offer her version of Beautiful, Beautiful Brown Eyes to the weekly assembly of the entire school.

Apparently her academic achievement was acceptable until the third grade, and it was before Thanksgiving that Mamma Lea was provoked to raise her voice in public after she saw Meritta's F report card. Faithful to Meritta's flawlessness, the teacher was reprimanded amidst endearing terms for her injustice to Meritta's efforts, "Honey, teachers now-a-days jest don't seem to understand that little girls has to play and can't stand things too hard for them. Besides, honey, when she grows up, honey, what's a young woman cooking and scrubbing to raise her family got to do with geography anyway." "But," the teacher interrupted, and Mamma Lea, perspiring profusely, face flushed, gasped and started another accusing tirade of the teacher's total lack of sympathetic understanding. The teacher was able to interject one more "But" before Mamma Lea, flustered, red and exhausted, stomped out of the room still muttering terms of endearment.

The two brothers, Artie and Allen, were four and five years older than Meritta. Artie was the silent totally conforming brother who had a straight "C" report card, came home directly from school and did his chores without prodding and suffered from a stammering speech like his father. Allen, who was a year older than Artie, was the unexplained character of the community who seemed to thrive on being the awkward unknowing adolescent to be teased by men and boys, ignored by girls, and patted by matrons. The unexpected aspect of Allen developed when he was in the seventh grade and his history teacher/coach told him he had to be on the basketball team because they needed his height. Ironically, the Lea property was the only one in the hollow without a basketball basket attached to the house or barn, so until the day Allen took off his boots and went barefoot onto the basketball court, he had never touched a basketball. He was clad in overalls and long sleeved denim shirt buttoned to the collar to hide the few hairs appearing on his chest. In due time the coach threw the ball to Allen who seemed to shy away from catching it. But to his surprise, when he shot at the basket he made it cleanly. It was not many days before he was the topic of conversation in the whole school because of his uncanny eye for making the basket.

The other item about Allen which was discussed widely was his refusal to shed his overalls and his only concession was to wear a jersey over the bib of his overalls. In spite of this, Allen continued to be a good player and when spring tournament time approached, his junior high team was expected to win.

To everyone's surprise Allen appeared for the first game of the tournament with the legs of his overalls cut off to mid-thigh length, but the team lost its first game. Allen blamed himself for the loss because his knees got cold.

None of his family ever came to see Allen play basketball and knew nothing of the jovial teasing the school gave him. It is also doubtful they realized some of his unboasted attributes as they related to some of the unusual characters in our hollow.

On the edge of the creek, opposite the lane in front of the Lea house, there was an unpainted three room house whose back porch had long ago been consumed for firewood. Pigeons and sparrows built their nests in the exposed beams. One Sunday morning a beanstick shaped grandfather and grandson nearing adolescence moved into this dilapidated house. They only unloaded a kitchen table, two cane bottomed chairs, a library table, one bed, one cot, three kerosene lamps, and two suitcases. There was no question in the minds of us and our neighbors that pure trash was now in our midst. In Appalachia, if a family moves on Sunday it is only because they are escaping from paying rent on the prior home.

Next day at the spout, we learned the boy's name was John and he looked to be of about Allen's age. He couldn't tarry to get acquainted with any of us because he had to hurry back to "Grandpap". All day long Grandpap sat in a cane bottomed chair propped against the clapboard front porch and read his Bible. Occasionally he would stop to spit tobacco juice at the chickens which strayed into their unfenced yard. And all day long John was busy cutting and carrying wood, collecting and burning debris, spading the garden plot, and appearing at the kitchen door with a massive pile of dirt swept from within. Each night the faint glow from a kerosene lamp would disappear by the time the smoke paled in the kitchen flue which protruded through a broken window pane. Then all was quiet until daybreak when Grandpap's Bible reading and John's endless work were resumed.

The following Saturday my brother suggested we take my marbles down to the lane to get up a game. No one intimated we had selected the lane for our game so we could invite the new John to join us, but by the time we had drawn the marble ring with a piece of broken glass, we were joined by three boys who were old competitors.

John was working at getting a hinge on the sagging out-house door when our marble game got underway. My brother and I were having a good day and our pockets bulged with marbles when we became aware John now stood on their front porch in front of his Grandpap. His face was dirty and he sweated as he told his Grandpap in a trembling voice, "I reckon I'm through now, Grandpap, 'cept for carrying water for our baths tonight." Slowly the elderly man marked a page in the Bible, restored his chair to the floor, and went into the house. He returned with a razor strap over his arm and a small notebook in his hand.

After removing a pencil from his shirt pocket and wetting the lead in his mouth, he began to read through small gold framed glasses perched midway on his pointed nose. "On Sunday, last, you cursed when you dropped the library table on your toes. The good book says thou shalt not take the Lord's name in vain. For this you must be punished with two licks. Then Monday morning, I had to call you twice for breakfast and that's another lick 'cause the Bible says I must be at my Father's work." He spat and John, now dripping with perspiration, interrupted. "But Grandpap, I never heard you the first time," he said. "Be not deceived, God is not mock," the old man said. "For trying to lie about it will cost you another lick." John stood silently and the old man continued, "On Wednesday when you stuck the rusty nail in your foot you were the worst of all. You took the Lord's name in vain and then cried like a baby. If you'd been wearin' boots instead of goin' barefoot, it wouldn't a happened and I wouldn't a been out three dollars ($3.00) for the doctor to get the nail out. You, of course, get two licks fer cursin' but I'm adding another fer ye to learn it's a hard cruel world and we gotta suffer through it like men."

I could see John struggling to control tears, and by this time the marble game was totally ignored as we all stood uncomfortably listening to Grandpap while the razor strap lay ominously draped over his arm. He wet the pencil lead again and returned to reading from the notebook, "Thursday, sneaked out of the garden while spading and jumped in the creek with clothes on. That's another lick." "I'll take that one Grandpap, it's worth it to cool off sometimes," John smiled. The old man made no reply.

"I reckon the coffee you spilt at breakfast this morning's jest worth one lick 'cause you did get up and clean it up. Now that ain't too bad a week, jest two, three, four, threes seven, eight, nine licks, but I'm warning ye son, if you turn loose of that post one time while I'm teachin' ye yer lesson for the week, I'm a'givin' ye four more licks, 'cause I aim to make a man out of you. And I'm goin' to keep on reminding you ye was born in a heap of sin without no daddy and with a no'account evil fornicatin' mother that run off and left ye when you was just a little tyke, and I've done the best I could by ye ever since."

John made no reply except, "Reckon we might as well get it over with Grandpap." As the old man slowly returned the notebook and pencil to his shirt pocket and carefully snapped his small glasses into a hard case, John began to loosen his overall galluses to expose his bare bony back.

We counted lick after lick as we stood gruesomely spellbound to the raised whelps of the strap marks and ooze of blood on John's back. Yet John clung valiantly to the porch post, tears running down his cheeks, but only a faint grunt could be heard above the resounding of the blows. Then it was over and John still grasped the post as he gradually wilted to the floor. The old man wiped his wet brow with a red bandana and said, "Now, John, fasten your galluses and we'll kneel and pray." At this point I left, forfeiting my remaining marbles, and my brother soon followed. At supper that night we related the episode to our parents. They both informed us that how other people raised their children was no concern of ours, nor did it become a concern for anyone in the hollow when it was realized this was a regular Saturday ritual.

Actually, one person did become concerned, but most of the neighbors didn't know it. One Saturday afternoon after I had made it a habit to play alone in the pawpaw patch to diminish the sound of John's weekly beating, I came upon John and Allen Lea. Allen was washing John's blood-stained back with a white handkerchief and applying salve to the whelps. Neither boy noticed me outside the playhouse the Lily children had built there.

By the end of that summer Grandpap and John moved away with their sparse household contents, and we settled into a less traumatic Saturday.

The other unique person in our hollow who reaped the benefit of Allen Lea's benevolence was old Dad Beaver. Dad Beaver had existed with his dog and two goats in a lean-to abutting an overhanging cliff down by the railroad section houses until a gift of a burned out trailer enabled him to squat in relative splendor in our hollow. Deftly, he placed a hand fashioned goat cart beneath the front extent of the trailer, and with intermittent urging whistles to the goats attached to the two-wheel, tireless cart, the goats pulling and Dad Beaver pushing, the trailer traversed over a mile to the entrance to the mine which was just above the community water spout. In no time, Dad Beaver cut a window in the front of the trailer, backed the trailer into the entrance to the mine, and like magic, he had an air conditioned home free-of-charge. He also had the additional bonus of an adjacent spring-house to keep goat milk and butter in the cool puddles formed from precipitation from the mine walls. Gradually he amassed enough rusty wire fencing and locust posts to enclose his goats and homestead. He made his living by collecting metals to be sold to the Japanese and these he hauled in his goat cart.

Contrary to the assumption that anyone who would squat in such crude facilities on unclaimed, useless land was "no account", Dad Beaver, stooped, silent, and appearing older than the hills, was honest, independent, and extremely energetic. Each morning I watched him rake his left over breakfast of fat back, gravy, and cornbread onto a rock to feed his mostly German shepherd dog, wash his plate and skillet before he set out with the cart harnessed to the goats to scour the countryside for lead, copper, and scrap iron to sell. Near dusk he would return to cut weeds from the creek bank to feed the goats, milk the nanny goat, cook supper for himself and the dog, and then rest on a legless over-stuffed armed chair propped against the trailer to enjoy a corncob pipe.

If Dad Beaver had any family no one knew them and no one came to visit. The adults in the hollow ignored him and complained about the "goat odor" around the spout, and as a result we children didn't visit either. Actually, Allen Lea was the only visitor he ever had and even Allen seemed to approach by degrees.

During the hot dry dog-days of August when the creek dries up and the minnows flop for an innate gasp of their gills in the evaporating mud, even the horseweed and dog fennel on the creek bank wilt in despair. It was then the goats began to nanny and chew at the roots of once green saplings inside their fenced lot and their rib cages advertised hunger. Allen Lea began to bring weeds from the fence row of their garden for the goats to enjoy. He then cautiously thinned the corn patch of stalks to feed the goats, so the goats survived the six weeks of drought. Allen justified his charity to Dad Beaver by saying it saved him more work, and besides, he was coming to the spout to get water anyway.

Gradually Allen began to tarry at Dad Beaver's when he went to get the family's "night water". On Sunday mornings Allen could be seen sitting cross-legged on the ground watching the old man trim his whiskers while looking at his reflection in a broken piece of mirror propped on the side of the trailer. Here Allen talked and laughed and awaited the high pitched, senescent chuckle from the tired old man.

It was not until winter that the billy goat died of unknown causes and Allen helped him bury the animal as well as help him fashion a modification of the harness to attach the dog to the cart. He even stayed with him all day to help accustom the dog to pulling the cart. In this way, Dad Beaver could continue his collection of metal scrap for which he received a penny a pound for copper and lead but only a fifth cent for a pound of iron. I was amazed that he could maintain himself on so little money, but he never asked for anything.

The only two times Dad Beaver ever left his house in the evening were when Allen was playing the final game of the basketball tournament the following year and the following evening on learning that Allen had been killed.

It was the year when Allen was in the ninth grade that he completed his adaptation to conformity and played in standard basketball trunks and jersey. Dad Beaver ambled around the periphery of the court while the tournament game was underway. No one asked why he was there because there were many older townspeople who appeared at these games because of the fervor of excitement which engulfed the community. The only spectators who remained in evidence were the members of the boisterous Dragon Club who had pledged a steak dinner to the players if they won the game.

Students and adults alike were standing throughout the game as it see-sawed back and forth. It ended in a tie, but Allen saved the game with an awkwardly executed foul shot.

True to their word, after the trophy ceremony, the Dragon Club carried the happy but spent boys to the Good Eats Café for their treat. Allen was, of course, the center of attention and was drinking a coke while he sat on a stool at the counter with the Dragons fanned out on the other stools.

No one was aware of men in booths in the rear of the restaurant. Suddenly a shot rang out and Allen was seen to spin around and fall to the floor. The drunks in the rear jumped up and tried to make an exit with one gun still smoking, but they were caught and wrestled to the floor to await the arrival of Peg Leg, the Constable. Unfortunately, Allen died immediately, so the Dragon Club members could only stand over him in stunned silence.

All the happy residents of the hollow that night had re-lived the game during their walk home by flashlight, and each family had quelled its hunger and excitement with a glass of cornbread crumbled in milk before going to bed. No one has to tell you some terrible tragedy has befallen when awakened to the shocked screams and the even louder cries for correction of the unbelievable, and the unwillingness to concede that the unanticipated has happened. It is a cry that, even before sleep is gone and consciousness reigns, one knows there is no hope that haste will undo the tragedy. And so, without need for communication, one dresses deliberately and listens carefully for the unquenchable grief of the bereaved to reveal a clue or the name of the member for which the community will join the surviving family in mourning. The futile barbaric motions of the wake and funeral provide a physical test of endurance to hide the idiocy of the canonization of the deceased, merited or unmerited, and the eulogy becomes a man's last effort to deny finiteness.

It was the wee hours of the morning when a deputy sheriff stomped his way up to the light in the bare bulb burning on the porch of the square, styleless house. As Mamma Lea related the next day after physical exhaustion from the round-the clock open house which wore the title of a "wake", had numbed her capacity to emote, "When that loud knock on the door woke me up, and I seed that sheriff's badge shining in the light, I thought surely Allen ain't done somethin' bad. Then when he told me Allen was dead, looked like I jest couldn't hear him. Somehow, even though I go in there and see him in his coffin, I jest can't believe it, and I keep askin' the Lord to forgive me fer askin' Him why He done this to us."

Those of us nearest the Lea home began to arrive as the doctor, summoned by the deputy sheriff, came to give a hypnotic shot to Mamma Lea and Meritta. The communal clinging and sounds of grief replaced words during that early stage of realization while we waited for the hypodermic injection to calm the most vocally distraught members of the family. Then, as though it had been prearranged, when Mamma Lea and Meritta were put to bed, the men and boys invited Daddy Lea and Artie out to get some fresh air, where squatting on their heels in the grassless yard, the disappearing moon could hide the unmanly tears, and soon a couple of neighbors would volunteer to accompany Daddy Lea and Artie to the undertaker's parlor to make the arrangements. Meanwhile, the women and girls were quietly acting as a reception committee to the steady stream of long-faced visitors bringing coffee, arranging hastily cut slices of ham, deviled eggs, and other foods to feed the multitude. Others removed imaginary specks of dust from furniture and turned mirrors and pictures to the wall. By the time the roosters announced the new day and the cows demanded to be milked, the bed in the front room was dismantled and stowed, and the house was ready to receive the casket and obligation flowers.

It was nearly unendurable to stand in the distance and watch the coffin containing the body of the awkward overalled adolescent be carefully carried to its stand in the front room. It is impossible to harness the thought that the gray velvet-covered, satin-lined box now contained only an inanimate object, no longer a person, but a thoughtless body, a form no longer requiring a repugnant shudder because it has been humiliated with an attire of unfamiliar black suit, white shirt, and blue tie. It is impossible to realize in the emotional impact of the bereaved family that a life snuffed too soon may be less dehumanizing than excessive longevity.

I don't know if the adults anticipated Meritta's attempt to steal the show when the casket was opened and the family stood hopelessly aware there was no reprieve to Allen's death, but all of us children swallowing repeatedly did. So rapidly did the silent Shirley Temple macro-tears change to the sounds too reminiscent of her earlier temper tantrums that Mamma Lea was soon noted to turn her caressing calloused hands from Allen's rouged cheeks to embrace Merrita and say, "Merrita, honey, if I could keep you from this hurt, I would. Try to be a big girl now 'cause you and Artie is all I got left." But Meritta's cries only became louder and her opened eyes looked nowhere. Daddy Lea whispered a stuttered request for someone to go get the doctor, but long before the doctor's arrival, a firm hand of a matronly neighbor had led her away and commanded three of us girls to help her build a playhouse beneath the curing hams in the smokehouse.

That evening after Dad Beaver had trimmed his whiskers a day early, washed the day's accumulation of dirt from his face and hands, he appeared at the Lea house in a new blue denim shirt and still labeled overalls. He stayed only long enough to shake hands with Daddy Lea and Artie, and stand wordlessly before the open casket a few minutes before he left with a bowed head and no apparent recognition of anyone present.

The school persuaded the family to have the funeral in the Baptist Church because it was larger than the church the Leas attended. It was a long and painful service but the entire community attended.

The drunks from the back of the café had been properly placed in jail and there was little interest in their fate. The trial would be so distant in the future it didn't rate concern at this time.

After the funeral the P.T.A. had a bake sale to pay for Allen's trunks, shoes, and jersey to be put in a glass case with the winged-

Atlas trophy they had won at the tournament, and there was a plaque which read, "In Memory of Allen Lea, Died December 12, 1936.

When the two drunks from the Good Eats Café came to trial, both were sent to prison for two years and this satisfied the community. After all, they both had become Christians while in jail and Allen had not been the intended target of their rage.

The Lea family had enough money remaining from the burial policy on Allen that they purchased a new Maytag washer which was placed on their front porch. Mamma Lea's Monday work load was thereby decreased, but that of Artie was increased because now he had to carry twice as much water from the spout to do the laundry.

As the gift laden Christmases, the Easter paraded fashions from the glossy pages of the Sears Roebuck catalogue were Meritta flaunted, and each Fourth of July watermelon was cooled in the galvanized tub, one of the holiday rituals of the Leas changed. Now they must go each Decoration Day to Allen's grave to leave jelly jars of cockscombs and gladiolas, and a wreath of crepe paper flowers. Artie and Daddy Lea must then mend the fence around the grave to keep cows from grazing on the mound. These same passing years brought Artie to high school graduation and enlistment in the army, Meritta to an ugly adolescence, only more age to the face of the always worried Mamma Lea, and an increased stoop to the back of the silent, workaholic Daddy Lea.

The attitude of the neighbors in the hollow about Artie's enlistment in the army was that this was better than going to work in the mines. At least if he got killed, it would be for a better cause than to stuff the pockets of the mine operators. It was usually added that the miner's union was no more interested in mine safety than the "bought off" government people.

It is regrettable that adolescents can't be imbued with the thought in a popular song of that time, "You got to accentuate the positive, and eliminate the negative." If anyone needed to accentuate the positive, even if it was nothing more than the word,"please", added to her vocabulary, it was Meritta. The bloom of adolescence had transformed her from the deck of the Good Ship Lollipop to a cowgirl tied to the burning stage coach awaiting the just in time arrival of Gene Autry in his big white hat. We knew each phase of interest and which heroine she would mimic because the loud volume of her Christmas present radio subjected us all to the whine of each western star bemoaning the loss of his little darling. Then as suddenly as the flattening tummy and budding breasts had brought the cowgirl transformation, it must have been the onset of menstruation which suddenly brought Veronica Lake into our midst. She appeared one Monday morning in high school with her blonde hair hiding one eye on her pimpled face. She stumbled in the highest of heels, and settled into the rear of the classroom to squeeze her pimples, pluck her eyebrows, reapply lipstick, comb her long blonde hair down over her eye, and read movie magazines when she was not ogling at boys.

Of course her parents still considered her infallible and catered to her every whim while everyone else knew she cheated on exams and laughed at her aspirations to movie stardom.

The remainder of the story of the Lea family is hear-say because I had gone away to school again. Meritta was finally given a high school diploma and got a job in a restaurant in the county seat. There she met lots of new people and began to date when a soldier would be home on furlough, but these dates only made her a more unreliable waitress and she soon lost her job. Eventually she got the courage to go on a bus to Cincinnati and got a job in a defense plant. About a year later, Meritta appeared at home at Thanksgiving time in a late model, squirrel-tailed, mud-skirted, dice dangling Ohio-licensed car and a male driver. It was not until her Christmas visit that she appeared pregnant and her "man" seemed only to grin continuously. When they left after the holiday their car was so loaded with canned goods, linens and quilts that the neighbors thought the Lea house must now be empty. But all that was learned at the water spout was that Mamma Lea was scared Meritta wouldn't know how to take care of herself and a new baby.

I learned in letters from my mother as the months advanced that Mamma Lea had become a daily worrier at the fence because of no word from Meritta. Daddy Lea bought Mamma Lea two cardboard suitcases and a bus ticket so she could go to Cincinnati to be with Meritta when she had her baby. Finally they received a telegram saying Meritta's baby had been stillborn and Meritta was very sick. An hour later Mamma Lea caught a ride on a delivery truck to go the three miles to the grocery/filling station/bus station. When Daddy Lea came home that evening, neighbors at the spout knew what to tell him so he went about his evening routine in his usual manner. During the two weeks of Mamma Lea's absence, Daddy Lea did his own cooking, packed his own lunch in his miners dinner bucket and heated the water for his bath in the boiler in the back yard.

After Mamma Lea's return home, her sad worried face was accented and she poured out all her woes daily at the spout. After there was nothing more to be said about Meritta, the neighbors would many times ask her about Artie's army career to divert her attention from Meritta. Her usual answer was that he was a corporal and doing something with dynamite but she couldn't pronounce the word of the specialist he was called. All she knew was that the explosives were more than a hundred times bigger than those used in the coal mines.

Finally the war was over and Artie was just one of many local young men to return home. They restlessly lounged around town in new civvies and white shirt with the sleeves turned up one fold above the wrists and made erratic attempts to find employment. Many of the veterans made bus trips to cities to look for employment and if found, they would return at the next holiday in a loud sounding used car and spend more time in the Good Eats Café than with their folks at home. In due time Artie began to date a shy recent high school graduate. After he was hired to manage the dynamite use in the mine, he was married to the girl of his dreams by the Justice of the Peace. They moved in with Mamma and Daddy Lea and each night both men did the slopping and gardening chores before bathing in the galvanized number 2 tub in the partitioned portion of the back porch. Mamma Lea still managed the household and the bride became a waitress in a restaurant in the county seat until she became pregnant.

Meritta, it was learned, had divorced her husband and moved to Detroit. There she was working in a Ford factory and saw lots of the people from home who lived in rooming houses near her.

Daddy Lea had a heart attack the following Labor Day while Meritta was visiting. Once again the hollow was awakened by the shocked screams and louder cries for the correction of the unbelievable. Again, the neighborhood rallied to carry out the "wake". After Mamma Lea and Meritta had received hypodermic shots and been put to bed, the men squatted with Artie in the front grassless yard. Finally a neighbor offered to go with Artie to the Undertaker's Parlor to make the arrangements while the women continued to act as hostesses and straighten up the kitchen after the large volume of food was stowed for later use. The matrons then sipped coffee at the kitchen table while discussing "how tore up Meritta was about her Daddy."

When the last shovel of dirt had been thrown on the grave mound of Daddy Lea, the ribbons were removed from the wreaths and baskets to be taken home. The near neighbors re-assembled at the Lea home to take care of the bereaved. Mamma Lea and Meritta. They were put to bed and coffee was served in the front room. An elderly, hard of hearing granny noticed Artie's pregnant wife and adjusted her corn cob pipe before she began, "Looks like you're goin' to have a little girl this time." When Artie's wife asked how she knew, the old woman said, "I can always tell. But I shore hope lookin' at that corpse don't mark it."

A young nurse recently returned from school spoke up, "Now, Granny, you oughtn't to scare her like that. There is no such thing as marking babies. All modern people know that." Granny defended, "I don't kere what you young'uns say, I know you can. My daughter, Helen, the one next to my baby, the one with the pig eye got marked when I was carrin' her. I worked at the big farm up the river bottom and was hired to cut the eyes outen the pigs heads they wuz makin' into souse meat. My eye commenced to itch somethin' terrible, and without thinkin' I rubbed it with my hand with pig eye juice on it. Sure enough Helen was born with a pig eye."

"Granny, that was a congenital glaucoma Helen had, and you didn't mark her", the nurse insisted.

"Don't kere what fancy name you call it, it's a pig eye, and I done it to her," the old woman insisted. It was obvious that conversation was at a dead end so someone got up to let in the cat of the Leas, and another lady thought she ought to get it some milk. Thus the gathering soon disbanded and only one neighbor stayed to help the remaining Leas through the night.

Meritta left the next morning and only Artie was seen around the house doing the morning chores. To everyone's surprise that afternoon, a well drilling machine was installed in the Leas back yard. When Artie went to the spout to get water, it was learned they planned to use part of Daddy Lea's insurance money to make a real bathroom from the back porch and have running water in it. Artie told the loafers at the spout that Mamma Lea had a bad heart and they needed to make things easier for her.

Very little was heard about the Leas for the next few years. Artie's third child had been normal and they were all growing normally. Mamma Lea required more frequent visits from the doctor and took more of the time of Artie and his wife to see to her needs. Finally, Mamma Lea had a stroke and died at the age of 56. All the hollow people gathered for the wake and funeral, but at no time was Meritta ever in evidence.

Mamma Lea's casket was placed in the living room and the whole town turned out for her wake. Not nearly as many attended her funeral at the Holiness Church, but there was a gathering of the neighbors at their house after the service. It was during this time the attendees made their comments about how well Artie's wife kept everything just like Mamma Lea would have wanted. Artie took a whole week off from work and the family took a short trip to Cumberland Gap.

Meritta hasn't been home in years, and now there is nothing to call attention to the Lea house and life goes on as before, except that now, all the families who lived in the hollow have a car, a telephone, and television.

Chapter XIV

Go Tell It On The Mountain

One of the fun parts of learning medicine when I entered medical school was to tag a diagnosis and apply a noble title to each of the complaints my neighbors taught me about in my childhood.

Our community was so close and so well informed on the ailments of each of its inhabitants that hypochondriasis, the smiling depression preceding suicide, menopause, complications of childbirth, and venereal diseases were frequently discussed entities expressed in our mountain vernacular.

One prime example was the pathologic museum of Mz. Keen who lived in the lane a short piece from us. She was always sick or pregnant, or both, and she always came to visit us as soon as she was ambulatory after a confinement so she could thank Mother for having my sister and me help with the laundry demands of her confinement. Each pregnancy made her so sick she invariably "walked through the valley of the shadow of death", and while she related the event in minute details, she chewed tobacco. Her arrival on these occasions required me to arrange her in a rocking chair and obtain a container for her to spit in. If the birth had been twins, and this occurred with every other pregnancy, even more arrangements were required to situate the extra baby on the floor near her. The baby which got her lap was the one crying the loudest, but as soon as she opened her dress front to expose her breasts, she went through a series of grunts and groans and we learned all about "the weeds". I never did learn how she came by that term because I never heard it in medical school or elsewhere, but there was no question she was referring to mastitis.

Some years we were fortunate if she had "freshened" in the summer because we could put her into a rocking chair on the porch and it was far more pleasant to allow her to spit over her engorged breasts and baby, than over the banister into the iris which filled our drip line in front of the house.

"I'd knowed all along it wuz goin' to be a curly headed girl 'cause I'd toted her so high, and for months I liked to a died with the heartburn", she'd say as she caressingly ran her fingers through the uncombed moist hair of the baby, and then scrape gingerly at its flaky cradle cap with a dirty fingernail. "But I swear to God, Honey, I believe this wuz the worst birthin' any human ever had. I done it all by myself and thought I'd bleed to death afore the doctor ever got there. But you know how old Doc Fox is; he's the best doc in the world if you ketch him sober. Anyway, I told my old man he needed to fetch old Doc 'cause all the life's washin' out of me. When he got to me he give me a shot while my husband was makin' coffee for him to sober him up. But, honey, was I weak! Next day I told my old man they should'a let me die 'cause I ain't goin' to be no good no more. Fer better than a week I jest laid there and cried. Well I knowed I oughtn't git out of bed for fourteen days, but after a week I jest had to get out of that bed and fix me a little bit of coffee, and I wuz craving some brown sugar and butter on a biscuit. Then just as I wuz swallowin' that first bite I was took with the awfulest pain in my breast and started spittin' up blood. It seemed like I couldn't get my breath so I don't know how I got back in bed. Reckon I wuz out of my head part of the time too, and I didn't even want no baccer to chew. When I come to, my old man and old Doc Fox wuz there with me and they told me what day it was." She then directed our attention to her ropy legs, one of which was shiny and swollen. "Well, they had to tell me what was happenin' to me, 'cause my left leg all the way up to my groin wuz just a throbbin' like it wuz a heart beatin' and it wuz all swoll so much the water wuz leakin' outen on to the sheet. But, you can hand it to old Doc Fox. He pulled me through."

During this recitation the baby had sleepily lost its purchase on its mother's pink nipple. Before she winced in cautiously replacing her breast to her bra ledge, the clean extent of the baby's suckling was seen clearly defined on the areola of the dirty crusted breast. Then the baby roused and began to searchingly grunt like a blind piglet. "Lord, I dread to feed that youngun again so soon 'cause I got the weeds so bad."

My sister and I had been in her house almost every day of her confinement to help her oldest daughter with the voluminous laundry, and many times we took milk and vegetables to them, but I had no idea she was so dirty beneath the surface, and I wondered how much that contributed to her complications.

In medical school I learned that Mz Keen had a postpartum hemorrhage, postpartum depression, deep thrombophlebitis and pulmonary embolus from too much bed rest, and mastitis without abscess.

The aura of infallibility with which we regarded the local medical doctor in our community would be enviable in today's climate of malpractice suits. If his treatment failed to work he was not condemned; rather, the end result was attributed to the will of God. However, there were some members of the community who either because of religious scruples or because of distrust of anyone who "had truck with the outside world" would not avail themselves of diploma doctors and relied entirely on prayer fests, medicine show products, or family handed down remedies.

Many school teachers of my acquaintance were regular users of Lydia E Pinkham's elixir. It seemed to take care of their "nervousness", menstrual cramps, and hot flashes. Of equal importance to the middle aged and elderly men, tonics and healing liquids obtained from the regularly appearing medicine shows took care of their joint pains, slow urination, loss of libido, and "don't give a damn feeling". The medicine shows provided additional entertainment for us all since they would have a variety of musicians who played spoons, banjos, or fiddles, and usually there was a stand-up comic to add zest to the assembly.

The use of slippery elm bark was well known to all, but I once had a hospital maid who had been badly burned when she was six years old. She had a universally scarred skin but her grandmother had treated her third degree burns with hickory bark. The burns covered more than seventy-five percent of her body and she shouldn't have lived, but apparently she was wrapped in the bark twice daily and had no deformities to prevent her from carrying on a normal life.

A conclusion I formed during my listening childhood was that the louder and the more varied complaints of the patient, the less dire the illness. When people get really sick they become silent and appear not to care about visitors, flowers, or the impression they create.

The scene which was the basis for this conclusion was the wrought iron scrolled porch of the doctor who was word-of-mouth advertised as being "real good in keerin' for the change of life." It was here the always complaining matrons of age thirty and upward awaited turns for a weekly shot which would correct nervousness, sweating, hot flashes, an uneasy feeling in the bowels, belching, pains around the heart, and a falling-out feeling. So graphic was the scene of the congregated women, gossiping and exchanging symptoms which acquired embellishments with age and experience, that even before puberty, a large note of skepticism already shrouded the event of the menopause to my way of thinking. When I voiced this skepticism to a rotund member of the porch set sitting next to me one afternoon when I went by to thank her for a chocolate pie she had brought me en route to the doctor, she replied, "Lord, honey, you'll be struck down with the worst change of life fer sayin' that. But I wuz jest like you when I wuz your age, and then after I had the youngun's I got so nervous it looked like I'd smother 'fore I could even git the biscuits made in the morning. But I sure wish you wuz right 'cause these weekly shots costs a heap of money and we already owe a big bill to Sears, and looks like every month we just barely pay the light bill so they don't come and turn off the electricity."

I asked, "When you get nervous with the change of life does it mean you'll have a baby? Looks like an awful lot of you sitting on this porch have had that happen."

"Lord, God, I hope not, but you can't never tell," she replied.

The following year right after the furniture company in the county seat reclaimed her living room suite, the rotund, nervous, pastry expert "took sick". To the chagrin of the shot doctor and the amazement of the community, an eleven pound baby boy emerged from her obese flesh and cured her acute illness.

It didn't require a Freudian genius nor a medical degree to form an opinion on this pathetic portion of our population. One had only to look at the leathery weather-beaten faces of these mothers of seven or eight children while no more than age thirty to know why they sought refuge in a shot. For the rest of her life, she would cook three meals a day, wash clothes on Monday, iron on Tuesday, shop on Wednesday, scrub the house on Thursday, bake on Friday, clean up the family on Saturday, and spend the day in church on Sunday. Sex every night was part of going to bed, and for most it was considered repayment for the husband's daily labor. With birth control so unsure in those days, the only change in her routine would be a new pregnancy, and with it an added burden and anxiety.

In recent years, the lay press and the federal government's department of health and welfare have extolled the virtues of the old family doctor whose bag was filled with babies and sparsely with real therapeutics. His over-hanging abdomen provided a prop for his folded arms as he dished out large quantities of psychotherapeutic platitudes and tender understanding. I searched diligently in my memory for a doctor with these ascribed attributes, and for a patient in my home town whose neuroticism had been talked away rather than being treated with a shot. There were no examples I could recall. Instead, I could only recall a doctor whose closest rapport with his patients was their shared knowledge acquired from the Reader's Digest. The added result of this long term hormone shot treatment was the number of these women who died of uterine cancer.

Moonshine production was a major livelihood for many families of Appalachia, and the market was always booming. By rumor, I learned some of the moonshiners were using carbide from mining lamps to make the liquor "work" faster. I never watched the process, but a few steady alcoholics in our community became ill with the Jake Leg.

I only saw one case of this in a man of about fifty who lived between us and town. He was in bed with vomiting and weakness for a couple of weeks before I saw him trying to walk to town. His right knee was twice its normal size and it looked like a bag of bones. If he didn't land directly on the ground, his knee would bend in any direction, and this frequently caused him to fall. He said it didn't hurt, but it was a nuisance to use his leg and a cane didn't help because he couldn't tell where to place the cane for support.

This malady wasn't mentioned in Medical School, but there was a similar condition called "Charcot Joint", which was one of the signs of third stage syphilis. There were several cases of third stage syphilis in our community, but none that looked like this.

Each year in early November, right after hog killing time, the odor of aspidium would begin to permeate every classroom in all the schools in Appalachia. Despite this foul smelling amulet worn in a tobacco pouch around the neck of the children whose parents swore it would ward off meningitis, the annual epidemic occurred anyway.

After three cases were reported in a community, its school, the theater, and all meetings would be cancelled, but the churches didn't close until there were ten cases with quarantine signs posted on the front door.

My parents weren't aspidium believers but my mother believed in keeping us home and busy so she would already be prepared for this event with a supply of scrap materials for us to make into hooked rugs, a jig saw puzzle to be put together, and a pieced quilt ready to be put into a frame to quilt. From the perspective of my siblings and me, we would find some way to make a sled and slip away to a mountain where we would be joined by friends who had already built a bonfire. We would pull our sleds up the mountain, slide down on our bellies, and then warm up by the fire before making another run.

The newspaper wrote lengthy articles on each epidemic, and the state health department sent workers in to keep statistics and teach us good hygiene, but it was difficult for me to put this crisis into perspective because death was with us always from cancer, mining accidents, tuberculosis, Saturday night shootings, and the summer "flux".

By the time the state completed the building of a meningitis hospital in our county seat, antibiotics had come into being, and so the building became an old folks home.

There were by far more small lives lost from the summer "flux" than from these meningitis epidemics, but no one got excited about the little ones rapidly wasting away from dehydration.

After acquiring some medical knowledge, I learned that meningitis is a droplet infection, so the value of wearing aspidium was in its odor--no one could get within sneezing distance of the wearer.

At the age of eleven I had a personal brush with mountain medicine as it was practiced in 1936. It was during the basketball tournament and when our team lost, my parents assumed my anorexia and vomiting were due to emotional factors. But next morning when I was no better they decided to call the doctor who had already taken Calomel out of his bag to give me when I mentioned my tummy was a little sore too. Fortunately he decided a little examining was necessary so I was sent to the hospital for an appendectomy. I was wide awake on the operating table and watched the two doctors scrub their hands and arms. They were clad in cap, mask, street trousers, and pink silk BVD's.

Years later after I had completed college and had a master's degree in nursing, I returned to this hospital to work in the operating room until time to start medical school. All my experience had been in a big university hospital in a large city, so I was ill prepared to see on my return to Appalachia one of the same doctors scrubbing his hands and arms while clad in cap, mask, street trousers, and pink silk BVD's. The one thing I didn't know before was that this same doctor always filled his mouth with a large plug of tobacco before starting to scrub. It was not unusual for him to slurp through the last hour of any surgical procedure and to see his mask turn brown.

Interestingly, I was the only RN working in the operating suite but the nurse anesthetist, who doubled as the director of nurses, provided some support for me when the practical nurses warned me that RN's never lasted there more than six weeks. She also assigned me to room with one of these practical nurses in the nurses' home because she thought I could keep her sober. I accomplished this for a month until her brother-in-law came to visit her.

He had brought a pint bottle of tax whiskey with him which they consumed in our room. When that was gone, I went with them in a taxi to a bootleg joint for a new bottle. Even though I was native to this country, I experienced an evening new to my knowledge. I had never been in a "wet joint" before and knew nothing of being frisked on entering "the back room" where the juke box was blaring, people were dancing, and a good time was being had by all. I even saw a broken beer bottle being used as a weapon in a booth quarrel before I lost my roommate and she didn't re-appear at the hospital for four days. She had to be admitted as a patient and required a couple of days of intravenous fluids to regain her normal state of mind. When she was re-established in our room in the nurses' home she couldn't remember any of the event, but she knew she had been found at the "Hortel" and that all the money she and her military husband had saved was gone.

Her summation statement was worth remembering. "Lord, God, ain't no tellin' what happened. I coulda got the "syph" or the gonorrhea, but I know I ain't pregnant 'cause I done had my tubes tied."

I had more experience in the area of medicine in Appalachia before I finished medical school. I had completed my junior year and learned a Baptist preacher doctor in an adjoining county needed a student to relieve him so he could take a summer vacation. The job paid thirty dollars a day and that was big, big money in 1949.

I would never be so sure of myself again in my whole life span as I was then. Even while I was driving over the mountain to the county where "Frontier Nurses" were famous, I realized I knew nothing about running a medical office, but I was sure the doctor would stay with me a couple of days and explain it all to me, and I was a little cocky about my home delivery experience I had obtained in school.

My arrival to the main square was at eight a.m. so the only place stirring was a filling station and garage. When I pulled in and filled my tank with gas, I ask where I might find the doctor. His apartment was above the garage and he hadn't left for his office yet they told me.

I climbed the stairs and knocked on the door, and was eventually told to come on in. I was told I should have known the door was never locked. The doctor, his wife, and two pre-school children were in the middle of breakfast in a disorderly kitchen. While I drank a cup of hair stiffening coffee, I learned their names and received the key to the office. Before I left for the office, I asked if he would be along soon because I didn't know anything about office routine. He assured me he would be along and show me the drug room since there was no drug store in town. (Later I learned there had been a drug store when he arrived but he dispensed his own drugs so the store went bust and he was able to buy all the stock at half price to settle the bankruptcy.)

The office proved to be on the second floor of the defunct drug store. The waiting room was filled with cane bottom chairs, the one table in the middle of the room displayed a pile of child riddled magazines, and the walls contained only two items to attract attention. One was a sign saying "No Credit", and the other was a print of the classic picture of the doctor musing over the child patient with red hair when the two parents had black hair.

Advancing to the other room which was office and examining room, I saw the desk piled with magazines and paper, an instrument boiling container was on a cluttered stand, but no autoclave was to be found. The only other items were an examining table and stool.

Further observations were precluded because two patients had entered the waiting room. One was obviously pregnant and the other a boy of nine or ten and his grandmother. Suddenly I wasn't so smart any more and began to sweat. I brought the pregnant lady into the office first and produced a large smile for her. Even before she apologized for being there I could see she needed medical attention because of her swollen legs, hands, and face. Her blood pressure was quite elevated and she had albumin in her urine. This was toxemia of pregnancy and could be fatal if not controlled soon, so I sat her down and told her all about it. We didn't have much to treat with in those days so I got out my little black bag and found some ammonium chloride tablets and dispensed this to her. I prescribed bed rest and a no salt diet and made her an appointment to be seen again in three days.

The grandmother and swollen boy then entered and the grandmother did all the talking. The boy apparently didn't have any energy and stayed on the sofa all day. I asked questions about how frequently he urinated and the color of his urine. She didn't know and he wouldn't answer. Finally I persuaded him to produce a urine specimen and sure enough it was full of blood. This was acute nephritis and there was no treatment except bed rest and try to get rid of his generalized swelling. The grandmother seemed satisfied and gladly paid the three dollars I charged

I was feeling pretty good about this hour of work because both patients had walked right out of medical textbooks and I had read my lessons. So before another patient arrived I went across the hall to get acquainted with the drug room. The one wall of shelves was full of gallon jugs of medicines and on some the label was not readable because of previous spillage of the liquid contents. There were big bottles of tablets and more liquid medicines on the floor. Now I was shocked and worried. I had never dispensed medicines before and knew nothing about concocting any combinations.

I was still roaming around the drug room when the doctor came in and told me I shouldn't worry about managing the office and dispensing drugs. He admitted he might not have written down which drugs he had used on the patient's card, but he always told his patients not to wash out their medicine bottles before bringing them back for a refill so I would be able to tell by the color of the medicine what he had used. He showed me three different colors of aspirin he had and where the Empirin #3 was located, but said the only concoction I'd have to make up was medicine for diarrhea for children. While I was still swallowing in amazement one of his children arrived and told him to come on to the car so they could get started. He did show me his home delivery bag and told me he only had one patient who might deliver before his return on Sunday, but even though she was the judge's daughter-in-law, she was normal and I shouldn't have any trouble with her.

He threw another curve at me after he had directed me back into the office. He had forgotten to show me his forceps for extracting teeth. I told him honestly I knew nothing about dentistry and wasn't interested in learning. He assured me there was nothing to it if I just remembered where the nerves came out of the jaw bones, but if I couldn't remember, just fill the area around the tooth to be extracted and nature would take care of it. Then he was gone.

I sat down on an unopened box and got out a cigarette, because I wanted to cry. What had I gotten myself into? Should I go on home and forfeit the money I'd earn because I didn't know about all these medicines? Surely the people would soon know how dumb I was. My dilemma didn't have a chance to last long because a man was pecking on the door and said, "Miss, I need to get back to work, so if you will just give me another package of these pain pills I've got the two dollars right here and I'll get out of your way." I took the envelope with one pink pill remaining and went to the drug room to try to match it. By the time this was accomplished, the waiting room was full of people and children, and I had no alternative but to try my best.

Fortunately many of the patients only needed sulfa drugs and I had already found their location in the drug room, so to add only the instruction to drink plenty of water didn't take long. Before I realized it, I glanced at the time on my watch while I was taking a pulse. It was almost noon time. My billfold was bulging with money and I hadn't made a note of any kind on a patient chart. What a way to practice medicine, I thought. If I had done this while at the University Hospital, every resident in the department would chew me out. I vowed to myself, I would get a bite of lunch and sit down and get organized before I started seeing patients the afternoon, but that never occurred.

The waiting room had almost been cleaned out when an overalled man with a red bandana bulging from his hip pocket walked in and said he was there from the jail and couldn't wait. I assured him his time wasn't so valuable he couldn't wait for me to see two more patients, so he sat down. When I had finished these chores, he got up and said, "Come on." My look was of total surprise when he added, "Didn't Doc tell you he had a patient in jail?" As I shook my head he filled me in, "The sheriff was arresting this man for stealing some clothes from a drummer's car and he broke and run. The sheriff pulled his pistol and shot him in both lags so he could bring him in peaceful."

When we arrived at the little wild west looking jail behind the court house, the jailor told me this wasn't a fittin place for a lady, but if I was a doctor, he reckoned I had to go. I followed him after he unlocked the door to the two cell jail with a key bigger than I had ever seen before. Lo and behold, sitting on a narrow cot in the cell which contained only one cane bottomed chair, a slop jar and a water bucket with a dipper, was a chicken thief from my home town. He recognized me at the same time as I knew who he was, so he said, "I know I got into your dad's chickens a couple of times, but they tell me you are smart and I don't reckon, what I done to your daddy will keep you from taking care of me." I assured him I would do my best and sat down in the cane bottomed chair to look at his legs. The bullets had obviously gone through the muscles of both legs and in one it had gone through the tibia, but there was very little inflammation. I even probed through the bone to see if there was still any lead in it. Finding none I told him, "You're a lucky man, and you'll be home before I am. There is no need for me to ask the judge to put you in a hospital so you can get out of jail. As far as I'm concerned you are fit to stand trial right now and see where you go from there." He tried to argue with me to go to the judge for him, but I stood firm. When I saw him two weeks later in my home town, sure enough, he was there and not even using crutches.

That first day of work was a long one and never a minute was predictable. After leaving the jail, I grabbed a sandwich at a restaurant and went back to the office to find only one man there waiting to take me on a house call. He told me I could take my car part way, but if I would follow him, he would help me across the creek. I checked the contents of my little black bag so I would be prepared for any eventuality since he was awfully vague about what was wrong with his wife of age 60. We stayed on the main road for about five miles and went for another three or four on a wagon trail before we parked and he held my hand while I stepped on moss covered rocks across a vigorous stream to his house just above the creek bank. I noticed several people sitting in chairs and on a swing on the porch and spoke to them as I entered the house.

The old lady was in bed in the front room propped up on pillows gasping for breath while one lady continuously wiped her face with a cold wash cloth. I felt her fast irregular pulse, listened to the rales in her chest, took her blood pressure and punched the swelling in her legs. I calmly told her she should be in a hospital but she firmly stated that was out of the question. She had to stay home even if it meant she would die. I loaded a syringe with medicine to control her generalized swelling plus the fluid in her lungs, and told her what to expect. Then I asked the lady with her if she would be with her all the time because I needed to give her some medicine to slow her heart beat and it would require someone to count her pulse because once she had the loading dose, the amount would need to be reduced. The lady seemed willing to cooperate so I explained about digitalis to her and left the room.

When I reached the front porch and the husband had paid me for the house call, a lady in the swing asked if I would give her a round of medicine for her little boy's pin worms. I moved things around in my little black bag and found the medication and gave the instructions to go with it. Without my asking, the mother produced two dollars for it, and then she turned to her companion to tell her it was her turn. Before I knew what was happening, I had a real clinic right there on the porch and had treated six patients. The husband then helped me across the creek and I got in my little Chevy coupe and drove back to the county seat to find the waiting room full of patients and all the ash trays full.

Those afternoon patients only got the bare essentials because I was tired and couldn't stand the mess of it all. But the very last patient was a ragged looking but clean young mother who told me first she couldn't pay me but her baby had the summer flux. The odor coming from the diaper bag made the diagnosis even if the wrinkled skin and parched lips of the little one in my arms hadn't told me. Now I had to concoct a medicine for this twenty pound infant and I had never done that before. I started with kaopectate, added some paregoric, and finished filling the four ounce bottle with cherry syrup. I instructed the mother to give the baby only boiled water to drink and give the medicine every four hours until morning and then I wanted to see her again.

Fortunately, I had a quiet night and fixed myself a steak I found in the doctor's freezer.

At five the next morning I was awakened by someone banging on my bedroom door. It proved to be the son of the landlady of the doctor's apartment and the garage below. And I learned he was married to the judge's daughter. He thought she was in labor, and her "water had broke." He waited in the hall while I dressed and I went with him to their house. When I examined her abdomen and listened to the baby's heart beat, there was no question in my mind she had a breech presentation. I asked if the doctor had told her of this and she and her mother were totally surprised. The patient hadn't had a labor pain throughout my long examination so I told them I needed to get some more supplies from the office and there was no need for them to start boiling water yet, so I left and went to the office. Even before entering the office I got my textbook on Obstetrics out of the trunk of my car and sat down in the office and read the entire chapter on breech deliveries. I smoked a couple of cigarettes while I sat there deciding if I should try to deliver her at home. Among the factors I considered in addition to it being her first pregnancy were that she was the judge's daughter, and I had never done a breech delivery. Finally I decided to go back to the house and see what would happen, but if there was the slightest irregularity, I would opt to take her to the hospital even though it was twenty miles away over a two lane road which was always in bad condition from the many coal trucks which used that road.

When I got back to the patient's home, nothing had happened and her labor pains were still very mild. I filled the bed room with supplies and sat down to time contractions and have a cigarette with the patient's mother. In due time, I decided I should get breakfast and go on to the office, but they could come get me if anything started happening.

The infant with diarrhea was the first patient I saw and there was a marked improvement in him. I felt pretty good and added some cereal to his diet. By that time, it was one patient after another, and I had already made a good reputation from the comments of the patients I saw throughout the morning.

At noon time I returned to see my patient in labor and her contractions were now the real thing. When I did a pelvic exam she was only slightly dilated and the baby was still quite high in the birth canal. But I'd had enough and wasn't going to risk the lives of mother and baby with an attempt to deliver her at home. I went into the kitchen with the husband and mother and told them I wanted her to go to the hospital and be delivered by a real doctor. They offered no argument and promptly got the county hearse/ambulance to the house. I forgot about the office and went in the ambulance with them over to the next county seat where there was a hospital. The bumpy road did lots for her labor and she was ready to deliver by the time we arrived. The doctor at the hospital asked if I wanted to deliver her while he stood by, but I declined. I worried while the nurse began to give her ether, and by the time she was asleep the boy parts of the baby were very visible. It was not an easy delivery but I was scrubbed up and helped. When it was all over, I thanked God, and went out to see the family with a big smile on my face. I received many hugs and a family of friends for life.

Before the doctor returned on Sunday I had made lots of money for him even though the one man who wanted me to extract a tooth was told he could have some pain pills to enable him to go to the next county to a dentist to have his abscess treated and possibly the tooth could be saved.

Even though the doctor wasn't very happy with my performance which I told him about while I was emptying my wallet on Sunday, he paid me the thirty dollars a day and he still had lots left over. After counting it he decided that if I wanted to come back on Tuesday for another week it would give him a chance to go fishing. I agreed and sang all the way over the mountain in the hour drive to my home.

The following week was much the same except that I did take time to make a few notations on the patient record cards. I would stay late at night to get everything neat, the ash trays emptied, and the cards filed in alphabetic order.

I saw only one patient who didn't have a physical problem and the husband came with her to present the problem. He was distressed because she read magazines while they had sex. I spent so much time discussing the problem with them I didn't get any lunch that day.

There was one house call which was upsetting. A girl still in her teens was only two weeks after having had her second baby. She was in a tar paper four room shack on the side of a barren mountain above the road. When I arrived she was reclining on a glider on the porch with her mother at her side. Chickens were roaming around the entire house and droppings were on the floor. The husband was drunk in bed in the front room and his father was in the same condition in another room. There were no screens on the windows or doors, and the entire house was a disheveled mess. Apparently the young mother had attempted suicide with the few pain pills she had and had cut her wrists in addition. Her mother had gotten the bleeding stopped in her wrists but didn't know what to do next. I suggested she take her daughter and the baby home with her, only to learn they all lived in that same house. I asked if there were a Family and Children's Agency they could go to but they said none existed. I learned they had been to the sheriff already, but he didn't want to do anything. In desperation I suggested they go back to the sheriff and have her husband put in jail and bar him from ever returning to their home again. I wouldn't let them pay me anything for the visit, saying they needed the money worse than I did.

I suspect that experience of doing general practice as a make-believe doctor influenced the remainder of my medical career. I wanted to practice a type of medicine in which I really knew my whole patient and the diagnosis. If I couldn't do the best that could me done for that patient, someone else should be caring for him or her.

Chapter XV

Let Your Light So Shine

We've each been given a set of tools

A formless rock and a book of rules

And each must make, ere life has flown

A stumbling block or a stepping stone--Anonymous

This platitude was enclosed in my diploma the first time I perspired beneath mortar board and gown in the hot June sun. There were no pearls of wisdom to be obtained from the guest speaker, whose curriculum vitae was larger than his vocabulary, but once that was endured, there was only the hand shake while flipping the tassel of the mortar board after receiving the treasured diploma.

Initially, my Mother thought I should apply to the Normal School where she had gone because it had become a college since her days there. But as the vacation weeks elapsed and school salesmen found their way up our holler to talk to Mother while I listened, my future changed many times. The worst fate which, for a time appeared to be my lot, was when a business school agent convinced Mother I should be an office secretary, which I could learn at home, and there would always be a job for me in the county court house. Part of the deal was for my parents to buy a used mechanical typewriter from him and also purchase his school's correspondence course. Our high school had not offered typing nor bookkeeping as part of its curriculum, so these would be useful tools for me to have.

It required about two weeks to attain about a seventy-five words per minute accuracy on the typewriter, but Gregg shorthand was another matter. It did nothing but ruin my spelling and introduce a feeling of dejection when my tutor returned my corrected papers with more corrections than I had ever seen before. Bookkeeping allowed me to acquire some basic knowledge but it failed to stimulate my interest. As the days flew by, I spent more and more time roaming up and down the graveled roads on my bicycle and dreaming of what life would be like in the outside world than in trying to learn the skills of a secretary.

Fortunately, a super-salesman from a small Methodist college only fifty miles away came to see us and convinced Mother this was the route for me. I would be allowed to work the second semester if my first term grades were adequate, and the cost was such that, with the sale of my cow, my father could afford to finance the remainder. Suddenly, Atee was at our house every day to get me ready for college.

In retrospect, this transition from home proved to be good because my only experience away from home, other than the two week stints with Atee, and a few sleep-overs with relatives, had been a miserable week in Lexington, Kentucky at the home of one of the Vacation Bible School workers who had stayed with us during her summer work. This experience was a real eye-opener because I learned I knew nothing about manipulating modern home appliances, and that my diction was so different that people from the outside world would ask me questions in order to hear me speak. As a result of this experience my ego was at its lowest ebb, and I could only pray that my fears of going to college would be quelled with time, listening, and watching.

I blushed while thinking of arriving at college in a one ton truck, but that occurred; and to make matters worse, Atee went with my parents and me so I had to ride in the bed of the truck with my Sears Roebuck trunk. Some of the embarrassment was lightened when I spotted a couple of high school classmates I knew, and I was assigned to live in the small dormitory with them. My only concern after that was to get my trunk into my room and the few store bought clothes I owned hung up without Atee opening the trunk for my roommates to view the load of feed sack underwear and orange and black dresses which she had made for me to display my school colors.

The only conflict which occurred early was my having to take a course in Bible which would not be transferable if I chose to go to another college the following year. However, the school's rigid requirement proved to be good for me because I learned about evolution and was thus provided an exit from the rigid fundamentalist religion with which I had been reared.

My two remaining years in college were at the state university, and before I graduated from the education college, I had a major in science and another in physical education.

The outstanding advantage of being at the state university was my exposure to music. Each Sunday afternoon there was a concert of some type, and for the first time in my life I could hear good classical music without having to hold my ear against the Atwater Kent radio to hear the New York philharmonic orchestra. Ironically, even though I had taken my clarinet to school, I didn't have the courage to apply to be in any of the school bands.

Except for my participation in women's intramural sports with a special interest in fencing, I was a loner the first semester at the University.

The second semester with my sister and me sharing a very small cheap apartment, I not only began to acquire friends, but thought I "had arrived" when I won the tri-state women's fencing championship.

My senior year was a happy one with my schedule of 22 and 24 hours. My physical education seminar was a project to work with a student who was severely handicapped with cerebral palsy.

In retrospect, nothing about the remainder of my life was planned. I did return to Appalachia for a few months after receiving a BS degree to teach in a mining camp school because of my mother's insistence. It was sheer fate which caused the gathering of my clan for a funeral, and allowed me the opportunity to go to Detroit and get a job in a Pharmaceutical Laboratory. After six months of feeling I was in heaven because I was on my own and at work learning something new every day, the factory nurse convinced me I should do something for the war effort and become a nurse. While I couldn't agree with her that nursing was more important than the assays on amino acids I did daily on the substance which was made solely for the navy to treat burns, I wrote for information from the two existing nursing schools which offered a masters degree in nursing for college graduates who were not RN's.

I was still only eighteen years old, and Yale University thought I was too immature to enter their school, but Western Reserve University accepted me. I wasn't their best nursing student, and my tenure was not without some strife because I knew more pharmacology than the instructor and there were occasions when I let Atee's rigid ideas rule my demeanor and so there were a few conflicts with my superiors. In spite of it all, I learned lots and acquired more insight into the whole world of medicine. Even before I had completed the school, I knew I belonged in medical school, but had no idea how I could find the money for the tuition and books.

Much of this phase of my life is mentioned in Chapter I, so suffice it to say that while I would have liked an academic hospital for my internship, I had to settle for one which had enough salary to allow me to exist since I was totally on my own. The hospital was named Woman's Hospital but there were a few male patients so the hospital could maintain a qualified staff in Internal Medicine and Orthopedics. Woman doctors were in the minority there, but a famous woman, Dr.Bertha Van Hoosen[4], who was the doctor in Petticoat Surgeon, had practiced there while she also practiced in Chicago, and before long I learned I was being compared to her, mainly because I would sometimes slip off my shoes in the operating room, especially if it was a hot humid day (hospitals were not air conditioned in those days).

No form of life is as demeaning as that of an intern, and mine was made worse because it was obvious I was a "hillbilly" and lacked many social graces. However, I impressed enough of my superiors that I was offered a residency in Internal Medicine and one in Obstetrics and Gynecology. I chose the latter in spite of the hard work which lay ahead because I felt I was good at it and was unsure if I was smart enough to be an Internist. The incident which made my reputation soar was diagnosing bulbar poliomyelitis in a post delivery patient who was under the care of my chief of Gynecology.

In the nineteen fifties, an intern or resident was required to be on duty every day plus every other night, and there were some weekends when work was non-stop from Friday morning until late Monday evening. During this time of slave labor, sleep became more important than food, and to find time to read journals and review textbooks required real dedication.

I learned during my residency what a terrible feeling it is to lose a patient even if that patient is acquired after she is already in crisis. On completion of my residency, I chose to decline two offers of

---

Brown, 1963.

[4]   Van Hoosen, Bertha, <u>Petticoat Surgeon</u>, Pellegrini & Cudahy, 1947.

partnership in Detroit and returned to Louisville to begin the private practice of Obstetrics and Gynecology.

My Chief of Gynecology had predicted I would never do another operation if I went into solo practice, but such was not the case. However, when I did my first major case, a ruptured tubal pregnancy, there were so many doctors in the operating room watching, there was hardly space for the circulating nurse to carry out her duties. It was then I learned that the three women doctors who had preceded me in practice in that city had never done any surgery.

Banks weren't interested in loaning money to women starting a medical practice in 1955, and my maximum salary as a resident had been three hundred dollars ($300.00) per month. I had completed payment on a reliable Chevrolet coupe, but there was housing, office rent and furniture, plus a few pieces of medical equipment that were a must to get started. Consequently, I signed up with the physician answering service to do house calls which paid five dollars for day time calls and ten dollars for night calls plus extra for any hypodermic injection given. In addition to this project, I also agreed to go to the office of a general practitioner who had been a classmate, so as to annex about twenty pregnant patients he had been seeing. My rent there was only one hundred dollars a month, but I barely broke even in the deal.

Yes, my first six months in practice were difficult because I only collected for fifty-eight percent of the work I did, but this was the type of life I wanted and I was not unhappy.

I didn't get paid for any of the teaching I did to nurses and medical students, but I didn't complain because it was a stimulus to me to organize my thinking, and I could see I was a better doctor for doing so.

It was not long before I realized many of the influences of my childhood were well ingrained into my being. There was no question I was a perfectionist, but this made me a better surgeon and drove me to exert more effort to make the correct diagnosis. From the comments I received from assistants, I became aware I had good use of my hands and I could only give Atee the credit for having started me sewing at the age of five years. Even as professional people became my patients, I found myself thinking I must treat this patient exactly as I would like to be treated and I found myself remembering many of the traits of Mz Lily who always seemed to explain things to me without making me feel like an idiot.

Worry can be a degenerating process, so to occupy my time in the office in the hours when there were no patients to see, I listened to drug detail men, read journals, and answered any phone calls which came in. One of these empty hour calls was from a lady who wanted to know if she could have caught leukemia from kissing her dead husband. When I saw her as a patient, I found her tiredness was due to anemia, and with lots of time to spend with her, I gave her all the iron samples I had acquired, and made out diets for her to follow to correct her anemia. She had remarried, and after her anemia was corrected, she promptly became pregnant. Over the course of the next few years I delivered six healthy babies for her. The thing which I remember most about her is that she began to include me in the Holy Trinity. The episode which occurred was a call to ask why her little boy had bloody snot coming from one side of his nose. I suggested it might be a paper wad or bean up his nose and she should take him to the closest emergency room to have it checked. After she had returned home with the child, she called to thank me and ask how I knew he had a bean sprouting in his nose. She went on to say, "You are the best friend I have, you, the Lord, and the Virgin Lady."

I also learned that first year in practice that one needs to get away from medical journals and the telephone at intervals so as to have a thought process and live in the real world. As a result of this I purchased a piano and took lessons, and also learned that sleep is much easier to acquire if a non-medical book is enjoyed each night. Even when, or especially when, a problem case kept my thinking fixed on it, I would review my textbooks and then open the fiction on my bedside table.

One day a sophomore medical student came to see me and stated he was fearful he wouldn't learn enough of my specialty in school. He would do any work for me free of charge if I would only teach him everything I knew. My retort was that any of the other twenty or so other Ob-Gyn doctors in town could probably teach him more than I, and while it was flattering to have him ask me, maybe he should look around more before committing himself to me. He affirmed he had looked around and I was the one to do the job, and so began a friendship which lasted a lifetime. I learned he had worked as a scrub technician for a noted hand surgeon in town and was quite adept in the operating room. To have him come at night when I called him was a real plus, and I soon learned he liked attending deliveries also. He did surgical dictations, hospital summaries, and finally histories for me. If I had an unusual case or an expected difficult delivery, he would call his classmates to get in on the action, and before long, I found myself lecturing for two or three hours at a time while waiting out a crisis or starting a surgical rarity. Such was the case when a single teenager with eclampsia (toxemia of pregnancy with convulsions) was referred to me, and for a few hours it looked like the patient would die. I had called in an Internist in consultation, and when he didn't have anything more to offer, I suggested we try to give her some salt free serum albumin in the hope of getting some urinary output and relieve her of fluid in her lungs. It worked and soon she delivered a stillborn baby and about three pints of old blood clot which had accumulated in her uterus.

After two years of practice I was asked by an established doctor to join him in his practice, and this changed my entire way of life. He was a close friend of many of the newly rich in town and his social life was totally new to me. For several months it was exciting, especially since my associate's wife helped me shop for more appropriate clothes and gave me the courage to buy a mink coat. They arranged dates for me so I could complete a table setting in their after hours entertainment.

The attorney who drew up our contract candidly told us a partnership is like a marriage except there is no sex. It required very few weeks for me to learn how true his words were. I learned more about that man than I had ever known about any man, and many of his traits I didn't like. I also began to realize I didn't like the superficiality and shallowness of his friends with whom I was supposed to associate. As a result I began again to take piano lessons and spent more time reading fiction so as to be consumed with something of interest when I wasn't involved in medical work. My other endeavor was to volunteer to spend a morning each week in the Planned Parenthood clinic in hopes of reducing the number of unplanned pregnancies in the disadvantaged population. It was not long after my work began in the clinic that I was asked to join in a clinical trial of birth control pills which had been preliminarily tested in Puerto Rico. It required very few months for me to become as enthusiastic about birth control pills as the manufacturer. After six months of use, I gave a presentation to the clinic board of directors and learned how Madam Curie must have felt when she presented her work on radium to the world. There were so many skeptics among the doctors on the board I was afraid I would be asked to stop the study, but they allowed me to continue. After a year there was so much demand for the pills from the public there was no way they could have been stopped even though there was an occasional pulmonary blood clot in those patients who were heavy smokers.

The principle change in my behavior while in a partnership I didn't relish was to return to friends of my earlier days. One was a secretary teacher who relieved in my office during the summer and her house mate, a girl who had grown up in the county seat in my Appalachia. She also was a teacher with a child and she was dating a reporter on our major newspaper. Not only did I enjoy their company and shared books and ideas with them, but I got to know several people whom I enjoyed. When my Appalachian friend gave a party for my substitute secretary before her marriage, I met the smartest man in the world. For the first time in my life I knew this was the man with whom I wanted to spend the remainder of my days. Eight months later we were married and my only regret is that he died at the age of eighty after we had been married forty-four years. He was a high school English teacher who lived with his widowed mother, and she was with us for fourteen years.

Our house was a group of old slave cottages and a dog trot which had been combined into one house so each room had an outside door. The four poster cherry wood bed from my grandparents fit in well with the few heirlooms they had. For many years we enjoyed collecting antique furniture and going to local auctions.

For the first time in my life, I felt I was a complete person. No longer did I dread going to parties because my husband was the life of all parties, and had a knack for remembering names. He was an accomplished pianist and knew all the old college favorites and jazz, plus he could play several classical pieces from memory.

After four years of living in the rented slave cottage, we bought a house built in 1810 by a Prussian officer who had served in the Revolutionary War. We got it for a song, and the bricks which had been made from clay on the premises required tuck pointing. My better half found some old brick and built an eight foot wall in the front and added some grills to set it off. Now we were shielded from the noise and very busy traffic of one of the major streets in the near downtown area of the city. Later when the house was added to the National Historic Registry, there was only praise for the tuck pointing and the brick wall.

It was soon apparent that my husband's students were as important to him as my patients were to me. While still living in the Slave Cottage, we would have all his college prep senior students for dinner each year because he was teaching in a blue collar high school and he felt these students needed to learn how to conduct themselves socially. We had only one rule to give when they first arrived--they could talk about anything they wished except other students. Each time the table was set with a full array of water goblets, shrimp cocktails in a container of ice, salad bowl, rib roast, green vegetable, potato, and a parfait dessert. We enjoyed the evenings as much as the students and most came to see us at intervals long after they graduated from college.

By happenstance, we began to acquire farms. One was only twenty-eight acres in the most prestigious area of the county, and it provided the facility for one of his students who, all his life, had wanted to breed thoroughbreds, to begin his career with the financial help of my husband. The next farm was acquired in an effort to ease the income tax burden, but it also turned into a big asset when core drillings for limestone resulted in a huge profit after four years of ownership. It was really fun driving to the bank to cash a cashier's check for more money than I had ever seen in my life. At each traffic light, my husband and I would bet a thousand dollars we would make that light.

The ex-student who was caring for eight brood mares on our first farm was given an opportunity to go with one of the big farms in Lexington, Kentucky, and my husband felt he should not be inhibited, so he quit teaching to move out to the farm to be available when the mares foaled. Obviously, this was not to my liking because if we lived on the farm it was a thirteen mile drive into town for each delivery, and it also took his mother away from her church where she went regularly and quilted with the other women of the Missionary Society. But to the farm we moved after we had a house built there because the concrete block house covered with aluminum paint was not adequate for our living.

By this time my practice was much too busy and we had only had one vacation in eight years. I was delivering between forty to fifty babies and doing twelve to fifteen major surgeries a month as well as seeing an average of fifty patients in the office each day.

Professionally, I had been reported in the local newspaper because I had been fortunate enough to deliver by surgery a very rare baby which was an abdominal pregnancy. Only one in several hundred thousand cases has happened. I really can't take any of the credit because the case was referred to me and I just lucked out.

The other professional case which had made me well known to the entire medical community was due to my conceit. She was a Jehovah Witness who had refused to take blood. Her doctor had dismissed her when she was seven months pregnant because she refused blood. Even though I put her on the most potent anemia correcting drug available at that time, when she went into labor she had an unusual amount of bleeding. But it wasn't until her baby was three days old that she really hemorrhaged. While doing all the standard treatment for the next three days, she still was on the brink of death. By this time there was no alternative to hysterectomy in spite of her 3 Gm. Hemoglobin. The unique thing about the surgery was that each little vein only bled cranberry juice, so blood loss during the procedure was minimal and she lived. When she was discharged from the hospital, my husband and I had a heart to heart talk, and along with his mother's unhappiness about living on the farm and away from her church, we decided to sell the farm and move away from the city. In 1969, we retired to Lookout Mountain, Georgia, but three months later I received a package with 28 cents postage due. It proved to be a book from the Jehovah Witness patient and was entitled, The Truth Which Leads To Eternal Life. I never read the book, and stated only that there is no way we can ever settle the score in that case.

We bought an ideal house which was large enough to allow my mother-in law enough space to be out of sight for hours at a time. In addition, her relatives lived in nearby towns so she would visit with them for several days at a time. Buddy, my husband, and I had a real honeymoon. We rapidly got acquainted with the neighbors, explored the surrounding mountains, historic areas, and art galleries. We even went to book stores and bought all the writings of authors we wanted to review and spent whole days just reading and discussing what we had read.

There were only five weeks in the five years we lived there we didn't have out of town guests, so I became proficient in shopping and freezing casseroles for emergency use.

Six months of this idyllic life swept by before my conscience began to bother me. After all, I was trained to practice medicine and I owed it to society. Initially I only conducted prenatal clinics in Public Health Clinics in North Georgia but I could see so much need for better medical care. Some of the doctors in Chattanooga learned I was living in the area, and asked me to talk to them. The following day I was director of the residency program in Obstetrics and Gynecology at the large county hospital.

I soon learned the program was on probation by the national accrediting group and many of the reasons were soon apparent. Hospitals are reluctant to spend money for items which will not produce revenue, and private doctors on the staff too frequently feel their only obligation to the hospital is to attend monthly meetings and totally forget the residents providing the extra pair of hands in the operating room and are entitled to obtain some knowledge from the hours spent in helping. Hastily, I began a series of lectures and began to assist the senior residents in the operating and delivery rooms. It required only a month to write an entire procedure manual for the residents to use as a rule of thumbs as they went about their chores in the emergency room and clinic. With the help of the departmental nurses, we set up some emergency packs and procedures to deal with the unexpected. It was less than a year before the morale of the department was changed and we then began to obtain applications from American medical school graduates.

I had continued to devote part time to the north Georgia Public Health women's clinics and their needs were still as acute as when I had started working there. Even if I rotated my externs and residents through these clinics, there were still emergency needs which couldn't be met. With encouragement from their Director, I began a series of classes and manikin sessions with all the clinic nurses, and set up a system so that the prenatal patient was seen by the nurses for two visits and a doctor on the third visit. They were also trained to do pelvic examinations and Pap smears so that physician time could be spared and unusual complaints could be dealt with. It required very little time for the Georgia Public Health Department to gather my lectures and procedures, and develop them into a now nationally recognized accredited Nursing Practitioner entity with an increase in pay.

My tenure as Director of the Ob-Gyn Residency was about three years old when the epic Supreme Court ruling known as Roe vs. Wade came into being. At the next departmental meeting I was informed it was my responsibility to establish an abortion clinic for the hospital, and I had until the next monthly meeting to give the department the details of it. Already I was receiving phone calls from the local news media asking what to expect from its eight hundred bed public hospital.

It is necessary to digress now to state that Chattanooga with its surrounding mountainous communities is an ideal place to live. Many things can be accomplished when the principle populace is well educated and all are civic minded. There were three private schools and their students were reared with the idea that everyone owed something to his or her community. Much of the original Coca Cola money was in that area and there were many foundations to drawn on.

At an earlier time, the public school system and Florence Crittenden organization had established a program with an outreach worker to recruit the patients so that all teenage pregnant girls were picked up at home by a school bus which took them directly to the Florence Crittenden Home for the day. Here they attended school, were given classes on baby care, a nutritious lunch, prenatal vitamins and iron, an exercise recess, and once a week, the school bus brought those with appointments to their special prenatal clinic at the hospital. This program yielded dramatic results both in the reduction of complications, and the prematurity rate, but also in the number of tax dollars spent on this segment of the population. There were only two school drop-outs and one repeat pregnancy in the four years it was in operation. Unfortunately, the American Civil Liberties Union caused a closure of the project.

Returning to the task of setting up an abortion clinic, I used the good rapport I had with the Florence Crittenden Home as I went about establishing the criteria for this clinic. I accepted the fact that babies available for adoption would soon not exist. I considered also that we must do what is necessary to assure that the genetic pool not become unbalanced. We must assure that each woman's future child bearing potential not be jeopardized, and I must not allow the time of my residents to be so consumed with abortions that they learned nothing else.

These criteria were fulfilled by having a graduate degree social worker from the Florence Crittenden Home do the initial interview and establish the amount of money to be charged. The resident then did an examination and necessary cultures and blood tests before he inserted a small device called a laminaria into the uterus so as to slowly dilate it. The next day the abortion procedure was carried out, and there were very few complications. This clinic persisted in this form until into the 1990's, when the nationwide demonstrators forced the hospital board to close the clinic.

While I was around the clock involved in achieving these major changes in women's health care in the region, my husband was involved in volunteer work, but gradually it became apparent he was not happy with the amount of time and energy I was expending at work. Even his increased involvement in learning water color techniques didn't fill the gaps of my absence. Cruises and exotic vacations of two weeks per year served only to reinforce his insistence on my total retirement. I had to admit I had "an all or nothing" temperament, so if we were to ever play, it was necessary for me to totally retire. The final factor affecting my decision was my increasing involvement in the political maneuverings of north Georgia and the state of Tennessee. I knew I wasn't adept in this field, and so we resigned everything and sold the house in order to move to south Georgia. Now my second retirement from medicine had occurred.

We made a bad investment when we moved to Brunswick, Georgia. The islands off its coast had no vacant houses in 1974, and Brunswick proved to contain only a transient population. We never got acquainted with any of the people, our house was unsatisfactory, and we spent as much time as possible traveling. By February of 1975, I had my fill of existing there and went to work for the only two Ob-Gyn doctors in Waycross, Georgia.

Many advances had been made in my specialty in the 1970's, but I found none of these in Waycross. My first assessment of the development of Obstetrics in Waycross was that which I would have expected in 1940. Yet, it was a beautiful community of azaleas and camellias, and the people were friendly and intelligent. Yes, there were some "red necks", but on the whole, I found it a small town worth all the effort I could give to improve the quality of life.

It didn't require many days to realize I had learned nothing about selecting professional associates to work with since my early experience in Louisville, Ky. Six months later, I rented office space and opened my own practice.

I not only had to teach my office personnel how to perform for me, but the hospital nurses had to be taught about fetal monitoring, ultrasound, and accepted up to date procedures. I felt like a missionary preaching except I wasn't teaching religion.

Secretaries with the ability to spell were a rare commodity in south Georgia, and so the problem was resolved when Buddy elected to manage my office and oversee the public relation aspect of my practice. Yes, there were a few raised eyebrows the first few days when he greeted the patients on arrival, but he was more polite and courteous than any male they had ever encountered, so it proved to be a good arrangement. It also relieved the old problem of filling his time while I was involved in patient care.

This area of south Georgia proved to be unusual in its interest in art. Soon Buddy was involved with a group of painters that met weekly with an instructor from Sea Island and not only developed new friends, but was motivated to continue with his technique in dry brush watercolors.

My practice was growing by leaps and bounds and more and more I was spending more time at the hospital than anywhere else. Even though I could sense some antagonism from some of the medical community, I ignored it and continued as I felt I should because I liked most of my patients, and it was no imposition to stay with them while they were in labor nor to be kind to them. Physical exhaustion was an ever growing problem even with my ability to sleep a couple of hours or recoup after a thirty minute nap.

Two more attempts were made to acquire associates, but neither was satisfactory. I even quit practice twice and gave the practice to the associates but this didn't relieve my obligation to the community and my phone was almost as busy as before. Old patients dropped by our house for advice or prescriptions so we made one last effort to carry on.

The event which changed our entire way of life occurred in 1983. Buddy had closed the office and gone home for his two ounces of bourbon and water and to open the mail, while I made my evening hospital rounds. When I arrived home, I was grabbed by a young white fellow while I was still in the car port and I heard Buddy say, "Do what they tell you." This didn't make any sense so I knocked the boy's hands loose and grabbed him around the neck while he blew stale beer in my face. All my Appalachian instincts were fully in effect, so I tried to maneuver him to an area of the car port where there should have been a lead pipe to hit him over the head.

A second young boy came out of the house with a fist doubled up and was rushing toward me. While still holding to the neck of the first boy, I grabbed at the hair of the second and at the same time kicked toward his groin. He was still able to give me a fist to the cheek, and unfortunately, I loosened my hold on the first boy, so he pushed me through the door and both of them jumped on top of me and held a knife to my chest.

By this time I realized Buddy's hands were tied behind him, and he was still begging me to do what they told me. I asked them what they wanted while I visualized the awful movie, The Clock Work Orange. They assured me they already had what they wanted so then they proceeded to cut a phone cord and tie my arms and legs while I remained in a face down position.

Their next move was to pick Buddy up and take him into the nearest bedroom and tell him to be quiet. After they made another tour through the house, they let our Welch Terrier, Twosy, out of the bath room and she came running to me. They instructed me to not try to call the police for two hours and then they left.

It required only a few minutes to undo the ties and go to Buddy to loosen him. I set off the burglar alarm but nothing happened, so Buddy ran to the closest neighbor for help.

The next few hours contained several policemen in our house and many questions to be answered. The burglars had taken only jewelry and money but the total was well over $90,000.00. We realized then how negligent our insurance broker had been in his evaluation of our assets.

Our burglary was the only news on all the local radio stations and newspaper for several days. I was fitted with a knee brace and went back to work the following day, but over the next few days our non work hours were consumed with our being treated to trays of food, flowers, letters of regret, and they made us feel we belonged to the whole town.

The boys were finally caught six weeks later in Phoenix, Arizona, and as they were being brought back home to stand trial, the policemen learned what a fine vacation the boys had at our expense. They also learned the boys had intended to dump Buddy into the river before I arrived on the scene and disrupted their thinking with my fight with them.

This episode convinced us it was time to retire permanently and have some fun. We traveled to many countries, sailed on twenty seven cruises, and visited all our friends who were still living.

When we stopped to consider how good life had been to us for so many years I found myself saying what I had said in 1965 when we were on our way to the bank with more money than either of us had ever seen before, "And think, this is little old Peggy Jean from Coalville, Appalachia.

Printed in the United States
52964LVS00003B/283-342